FROM PERRY GUTTER TO BIRMINGHAM

FROM PERRY GUTTER
TO BIRMINGHAM
The Story of a Shropshire Girl

Connie Hayball

Shoestring Press

Printed by imprintdigital
Upton Pyne, Exeter
www.imprintdigital.net

Typeset by Nathanael Ravenlock
nat@ravenlock.eu

Published by Shoestring Press
19 Devonshire Avenue, Beeston, Nottingham, NG9 1BS
(0115) 925 1827
www.shoestringpress.co.uk

First published 2011
© Copyright: Connie Hayball
The moral right of the author has been asserted.
ISBN 978 1 907356 20 9

About the Author

Connie Hayball is the only remaining child of Hilda Pressdee, whose life is recounted in this book. Connie was brought up in Birmingham and attended Birmingham University, after which she became an English teacher in secondary schools, settling in Leicestershire. Her parents were both socialists and Connie and her husband were also active politically, being members of the Labour Party for many years. In retirement Connie and her husband were members of the University of the Third Age and the local Pensioners' Action Group. Now widowed, Connie continues these interests, and enjoys spending time with her family – a son and daughter, and three grandsons.

Contents

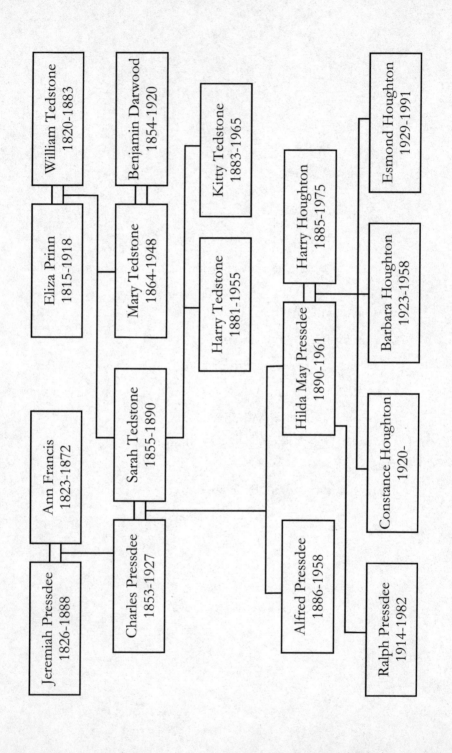

Preface

This book tells the story of the life of my mother Hilda May Pressdee, and her family and friends. They were not famous or distinguished; they were ordinary people who endured hardship, poverty and loss. They encountered premature deaths, unemployment, disease, overcrowding and war. But there was also love, family support, friendship, and – yes – fun. And as the twentieth century proceeded, liberal and political action resulted in an amelioration of the lot of working people, which at the beginning of the century could hardly have been imagined. Ordinary people sometimes live extraordinary lives. I think my mother was one of them.

By the time she was two years old Hilda had neither father nor mother to care for her. Her nearest relative, her mother's sister, would have taken in the two parentless children (Hilda and her brother Alf) but with a young family of her own, and living in a small house, was unable to do so. Hilda and Alf therefore had to be placed in a workhouse orphanage, where they spent their childhoods. In spite of this inauspicious beginning, and the tribulations of her early life, Hilda established a happy family home, with four children, three of whom went to grammar school and two of whom became university graduates. She was for many years a member of the Cooperative Women's Guild, and as a socialist attended the funeral of the first leader of the Communist Party of Great Britain, Harry Pollitt.

She married a man who shared her left wing views, and though sometimes stormy, the marriage endured. During her last years they went on several holidays, including Ireland and the Isle of Man. She showed great courage during the Second World War, being out with an ambulance throughout the blitz on the city of Birmingham. She was a devoted grandmother and loved having her grandchildren to stay in her home.

What follows is a tribute to a woman who overcame many difficulties with courage and endurance. It is a work of love written by her surviving daughter. The references to railway journeys are the work of my son Dick, as is also the cover illustration, and much of the research has been undertaken by my daughter, Jane. Background information has been supplied by the Shropshire Archives and the Shropshire Regimental Museum, and taken from the books listed in the bibliography. The articles about the Clun Poor Law Union by Alan Goff in the *South West Shropshire Historical and Archaeological Journal* have proved especially useful. Local historians from Bishops Castle (Judith Pearce and Prue Dakin) and Hopesay (Sandra Spence) have also provided very valuable information. I would like to thank all these, and especially my daughter, without whose unstinting help much of this book could not have been written.

Chapter 1: Introduction

My daughter Jane and son Dick and I visited Bishops Castle in September 2009 with the aim of discovering all we could about the childhood of my mother, Hilda May Pressdee. Why, when her father and grandmother were still alive, was she brought up as an orphan in Bishops Castle workhouse? What was life like in the workhouse? What might have been lacking in her childhood?

We found we had stumbled upon a week of celebration in the town: it was Michaelmas weekend. We decided to postpone our investigations and join in the fun. And fun it was. There was a craft fair, an antiques fair, a farmers' market, and many attractions for children. The church had an exhibition of local art (and coffee and cake obtainable), the college of further education presented an exhibition of old musical instruments, in which someone was playing a dulcimer, bands performed in front of the Town Hall almost continuously, we found a pub in which a blues group was playing in the garden, and museums and exhibitions were open to the public. Best of all, on both days a procession of old vehicles proceeded down the main street: tractors, cars, buses, driven by men (and some women) who looked as old as the vehicles! Pubs and cafes were open all day, but throughout we never saw an example of what we now call "anti-social behaviour". This made us think that surely a workhouse in this town could not have been as miserable as Dickens presented them.

We know that in fact Mum was not always miserable as a child: her stories to me indicated that. Nevertheless, life for children in such circumstances must have lacked the one thing that all children need – love. This was brought home to me recently when Gordon Brown apologised for the mistreatment of children from broken homes who were sent to Australia after the Second World War. Some of those children, now in their fifties, were interviewed on television. One man put his finger on the worst thing that happened to them – "There was no love", he said.

Chapter 2: Hilda is born in Perry Gutter

Mum was born in 1890 on April 12th. She believed her birthday was April 1st for most of her life and discovered the truth only when she applied for her old age pension when she reached sixty. Her aunt, known to me as "Auntie Darwood" and to my mother as "Auntie May", had told her that she was born at the beginning of April. But no one had ever given her the correct date. If they had she would have been spared much teasing for having been born on April Fools' Day.

She was, in her own words, a "proud Salopian". She did not seem to be aware that northern Shropshire was the birthplace of the industrial revolution, but she did know that Captain Webb, the first man to swim the English Channel (in 1875), was from Shropshire, and she often spoke about him, and how he met his end. He took his daring too far, as she told me, by attempting in 1883 to go over the Niagara Falls in a barrel. However, I later found that she had given me incorrect information and he had in fact tried to swim across the river beneath the falls. Although this was seven years before Hilda was born, his exploits remained popular for many years, with large numbers of commemorative items produced in the county and Bryant and May matchboxes featuring a picture of him. In 1909 a memorial to him was unveiled in his birthplace – Dawley – and would have attracted widespread publicity.

Hilda left Shropshire at the age of fourteen, after a childhood in the workhouse, and the rest of her life was spent in cities. Her fondness for Shropshire must have been in part because that was where she knew she once had a home and parents – the "land of lost content" such as that described by Housman in "A Shropshire Lad".

Hilda's birth took place in a cottage in a small hamlet called Perry Gutter. We found this place just outside Hopesay. Hopesay is a small village about one mile north of Aston-on-Clun and some seven miles south east of Bishops Castle. The village is overlooked by an Iron Age fort on Burrow Hill, and to its northwest there is an Iron Age settlement at Wart Hill. Apart from its church it has no facilities, and the unclassified road running through the village gets little traffic. The surrounding area is beautiful, and the whole district is now classified as an area of outstanding beauty, with Hopesay Hill having come into the possession of the National Trust in 1952.

Perry Gutter is a short distance from Hopesay village. At the entrance we found a sign on the open gate, which said "Private Road". There was a small track, which wound up the hillside, until we suddenly came within sight of a fairly substantial house with large windows and a porch. Its three chimneys, however, placed equidistant from each other, together with the brickwork, suggested that this had once been several cottages. This, then, was Perry Gutter, and it might have been in one of those cottages that now formed this house that Mum was born. I had thought Perry Gutter was the name of a street in Hopesay, for the hamlet is actually in the parish of Hopesay, but my assumption was wrong. A footpath used to lead from Perry Gutter to Hopesay – it was stopped up in 1905 by a local landowner and a new one created – and it seems likely that footpaths were the only access when Hilda's parents lived there. Another footpath went through the fields down to Aston-on-Clun. The derivation of the hamlet's name is not known, but "Perry Barr" – a part of Birmingham – means 'small hill' (from the Latin 'parva'), and although there are other possibilities for 'Perry' (a version of the Welsh "ap Herry" – son of Henry – or linked to pears) it seems likely that the 'perry gutter' was the small stream which still flows near the cottages, down through the field to join another stream that runs between Hopesay and Aston-on-Clun.

The view from Perry Gutter

There were eight dwellings in Perry Gutter when the 1891 census was taken (four having four rooms, and the other four three rooms), but by 1901 only three dwellings were occupied. We don't know the origins of the homes but they were probably fairly roughly built cottages originally leased to people who worked for the local landowners (either on the land or as domestic servants). In the earlier nineteenth century there were consistent concerns about squatters in areas just outside the village, including Perry Gutter, so it seems that the area may have initially developed as a place occupied by the poor. *Beddoes Connection in Hopesay* notes that the so-called "problem" of the poor is included in several archive sources in the 1800's. In 1804 the new rector Rev John Hardinge had taken the initiative to get an agreement between the Lord of the Manor and freeholders to enclose 160 acres on Hopesay Hill because of his concern to see the "immoral dwellers" cleared of the common. It is also noted that in 1841 there were people in cottages above the waste (meaning the common) who were "terrible sheep and pony stealers", many living idly, and the 1851 census records families living in turf cottages and tents on the common. The area of Perry Gutter and the hillside above was particularly notorious for squatters – rather different from the attractive house that now occupies this spot. Hilda's grandfather William Tedstone (and his mother and siblings) are first recorded as living in Perry Gutter on the 1851 census, so the family had probably been there for forty years by the time Hilda was born.

Mum and her twin Charles were the last children born to Sarah Pressdee (1855–1890). Sarah's eldest children, known to me as Uncle Harry and Auntie Kitty, were illegitimate. While Harry was born in Hopesay in 1881, Kitty was born two years later in a village near Bridgnorth, where Sarah was working as a domestic servant, so undoubtedly Harry was being looked after by the family in Perry Gutter. On 2nd August 1887 Sarah married my grandfather, Charles James Pressdee, a former soldier, who was at the time of Mum's birth working as an agricultural labourer. There were two surviving children of this marriage – Mum, and my Uncle Alf who was three years her senior. Alf, who was born in 1886, was in fact also illegitimate but Charles Pressdee acknowledged him as his son, and Alf certainly regarded him as his father. Alf was registered after birth with his mother's maiden name – Tedstone – but we only ever knew him as Alf Pressdee, and he used this surname all his life.

Both Alf and my mother were twins. Alf's twin Florence survived for five months and died at the end of December 1886. Hilda's twin – a boy, named Charles after his father – also survived for five months, but at his death in September 1890 had been weakening for over two months. He was christened on 22nd July in Hopesay when, presumably, it was thought that he was unlikely to survive (Hilda was not christened until the following year which suggests that his christening was hurriedly arranged). Mum was aware that both she and Alf had been twins, but thought that the other babies had died at birth. Research into infant mortality levels in the nineteenth century has shown that although levels could be high in industrialised areas, rural areas also experienced high levels, often concentrated in small pockets where infant mortality rates could match those of the most overcrowded and unhealthy areas of the cities. Medical Officer of Health reports for Shropshire in the latter part of the century highlighted poor sanitation and drinking water quality and a shortage of trained midwives as key factors. It certainly appears that the Tedstone family in Perry Gutter experienced a significant number of child infant deaths: Sarah's mother Eliza had at least three children who died within weeks of birth, and two of Sarah's aunts also lost babies within weeks of birth.

It must have been a hard life, and a daily struggle in a cramped cottage with none of the facilities that we have today – no piped water, gas or electricity. Fresh water would have been obtained from the stream, or could have been taken from the village pump in Hopesay on occasion, and rainwater for washing would probably have been collected in a barrel. Sanitation was primitive: there would have been a sump or pit in the ground to take waste.

We do know that there was a fireplace, so presumably the inhabitants could keep warm to some degree, though they are more likely to have burnt wood than coal, and such cottages were usually very damp. All in all, a very basic provision of the necessities of life. Light would have been from candles – they were unlikely to have had oil lamps – which would probably have been purchased by Charles on his weekly shopping trips. The winter of 1886 was exceptionally severe, with fierce gales and snow over much of England. Conditions in the cottage, with one of the first twins probably fairly clearly near to death, would have been correspondingly hard.

My mother's maternal grandmother, Eliza Tedstone (née Prinn) was also living in the cottage, a formidable and resourceful woman. She was a widow on whom much responsibility for her daughter's family was to fall. Her husband William had died in 1883, by which date Sarah already had two illegitimate children, whom Eliza undoubtedly looked after while Sarah worked. Eliza herself had been orphaned at birth and raised by another family. How she made her way to Hopesay (from the Shrewsbury area where she was brought up) is not clear, but along the way she had at least two illegitimate children before marrying William Tedstone, and a total of thirteen children altogether (although we only have any evidence of four surviving much beyond babyhood). She was allegedly born in the year of the battle of Waterloo – 1815 – and was awarded a prize of five guineas in 1917 for being the oldest resident of Ladywood, Birmingham. When she died in 1918 the *Birmingham Mail* carried an obituary notice, which gave her age as a hundred and three, and stated that she could still read the *Birmingham Mail* without glasses. Mum used to laugh about this for the old lady couldn't read or write! Mum also told me that Eliza had walked over the Wrekin at the age of seventy – a story which must be apocryphal or confused, for at that stage of her life she lived at the other end of the county, and subsequently in Birmingham. However, as Eliza came originally from Shrewsbury in the north of the county, she may well have been familiar with the Wrekin, and the story was no doubt embroidered as she grew older. To go "all around the Wrekin" is a local phrase to describe someone who has gone a long way around something, and one often used by my mother. Eliza may perhaps have felt that moving to Birmingham at the age of over seventy, and having gone from Shrewsbury to Hopesay when a young woman, was in some senses going "around the Wrekin".

Sarah died on 18 May 1890, five weeks after my mother's birth. Her death certificate states that she had suffered bronchitis and congestion of the lungs for three weeks, dropsy and general exhaustion. The family said that she had suffered puerperal fever, which my mother always told me had been the cause of death, and I imagined that she had died shortly after the birth of the twins. Those five weeks before her death with two new babies needing care must have been a terrible time for them all. The local medical practitioner – Danby Browne, a single man from Ireland – certified the death, but was clearly not able to do anything to prevent what appears to have been primarily caused – like so many deaths at that time – by impoverished and harsh living conditions. Most labouring families were unable to afford the fees for midwives or doctors, and it is likely that Sarah gave birth to the twins with only the support of her mother and perhaps a neighbour. That her death was certified by a doctor suggests that the family were so desperate that they used much needed savings or other resources to pay for his attendance, or, more likely, that he was paid by a charitable source or a local friendly society (if Charles was a member) to visit Sarah.

Chapter 3: Father Charles is now in charge

Now, in the cottage on the hill, Charles Pressdee had to provide for the penniless old lady, Eliza, as well as five children: Harry, Kitty, Alf, and the new twins, Hilda and Charles. The tiny three-roomed cottage must have been very cramped. However, at some stage before April 1891 we know from the census records that both Kitty and Harry had moved to live with relatives. Charles kept his own children, with his mother-in-law looking after them for him. Whether the departures of the older children took place before Sarah's death or after we do not know – either option seems feasible, with the wider family helping out the Perry Gutter relatives who were clearly having a difficult time even before Sarah's death.

Harry (aged eight when his mother died) went to his great-aunt Martha in Wolverhampton. Martha Tedstone (born 1835) was the youngest sister of William Tedstone (Eliza's deceased husband and Sarah's father). She was fifteen years younger than William, born after their father's death, and it seems likely that William played a fatherly role in her life, as he continued to live with his mother and siblings, and subsequently his step-father. The family moved from Aston into a cottage in Perry Gutter when Martha was a child, and she was based there (although working away for some of the time) until she married William Jones in Staffordshire in about 1874. Before that, however, she had at least three illegitimate children and the two surviving sons (Robert, born in 1862, and Thomas, born in 1867) lived with William and his family in Perry Gutter, growing up alongside his daughters Sarah (my grandmother) and May. Although Martha and her husband had two younger daughters and also Thomas living with them by 1891, they nevertheless took in Harry, Sarah's eldest son. Times were perhaps a bit better for Martha: her husband had been a groom but was now a "carter working for the corporation" – presumably regular employment – and they also had a lodger. She probably felt it was now her turn to help her deceased brother's family, as he had helped her.

Kitty, who was six when Sarah died, was taken in by Sarah's sister May (Auntie Darwood) and her husband Ben in Birmingham. May and her husband also gave continuing support to the family, as well as taking Kitty into their home.

My mother cannot have known what life was like at this time, for she was only a baby. Alf remembered little of it, for he was only three and a half years old when his mother died. However, my mother recalled things that someone, probably her grandmother Eliza, told her. Mum knew her grandmother in later years (at one time during the First World War they were both living in the same house) so it seems likely that she would have told Mum tales of her early childhood. Mum knew, for instance, that she was reared on Nestle's baby milk. She remembered, too, what she had been told about her father, whom, as we shall see, she never knew. She always told me that he had been "a redcoat" – no doubt she liked the idea better than calling him a common soldier, which he was. A very clever man "They couldn't teach him any more at the village school", she used to say, "he had learnt all they knew". Well, maybe. The only sign of cleverness that I can find in his army record is that when he enlisted at the age of twenty-two he gave his religion as "Episcopalian". Who were they? There was no such church in the vicinity of his home. Recruits often gave unlikely religious denominations in order to avoid church parade on Sundays. His younger brother Alfred, who enlisted a year after

Charles, gave his religion as Church of England. Which sounds more like it.

Charles and Alfred were the sons of Jeremiah Pressdee (1826-1888), a master shoemaker. Shoemaking was then still a cottage industry in many places. A large proportion of the rural population worked in traditional crafts. In 1852 18% of the rural male population aged 20-64 was employed in ten major trades and crafts: baker, blacksmith, bricklayer, butcher, carpenter, mason, publican, shoemaker, shopkeeper and tailor. Jeremiah had married a local girl, Ann Francis, from Newcastle on Clun (about ten miles from Hopesay) and his eldest son Charles James was born in January 1853, in Hopesay. Ann's family, too, worked in a local trade – her father and brothers were wheelwrights, making waggons. At that time they seem to have been fairly prosperous and both Ann's father and most of her brothers were master wheelwrights employing other men. Large horse-drawn waggons were essential to Victorian farming, later to be replaced by tractors and other machinery. In *The Farm Waggons of England and Wales* there is a picture of a waggon made in about 1880 by Francis of Newcastle on Clun.

Charles was trained to work in his father's trade. At age 18 in 1871 he was living at home, in a small cottage called "Birches", and working as a shoemaker. In the 1863 Post Office Directory for Hopesay Jeremiah is listed as a shopkeeper at Birches (presumably selling shoes), and the various locations in the parish are described. Perry Gutter and its residents are not included. When Charles joined the army in 1877 his occupation is noted as "boot closer" (confirming that he worked with others, as this is just one part of the boot-making process, traditionally done by a relative of the shoemaker). After he left the army, however, he is only shown on records as a farm labourer – it appears that he did not go back to shoemaking.

By this time it seems that his father Jeremiah had also left this trade, and also Hopesay. The first shoe factories in England were established in the 1850's and by the 1860's were using a range of machines for various stages of the processes. Over the next few decades the makers of hand-sewn shoes were gradually squeezed out of business, and eventually by the time of the First World War most village shoemakers had become repairers. In addition, by the 1880's large amounts of ready-made footwear were being imported from America. The last trace we have of "Birches" (which was a single cottage in a field near to Perry Gutter) is on the death certificate of Charles' mother, who died there in 1872. Army records of next of kin show Jeremiah to be living in Wales in 1877. By the time of the 1881 census both Charles and his brother Alfred were in the army, their two sisters were in North Wales, and their father and younger brother William were staying with relatives in Morville (also in Shropshire). When Jeremiah died in 1888 he had been working as a foreman at a chemical works in Dudley, clearly having abandoned shoemaking. Census returns of occupations chart the declining numbers of boot and shoe makers in the nineteenth century – in 1851 there were 274,451 boot and shoe makers but by 1871 this has reduced to 223,365. The family history therefore suggests to us that when Charles left his regiment in 1884 (when he joined the reserve) he had neither a family home nor a trade in Hopesay to which he could return. He did, however, go back there and resume his acquaintance with his future wife, whom he had known from childhood when they had grown up in cottages in neighbouring fields.

Mum told me that on Saturdays her father used to buy the week's groceries for the family. He didn't, however, arrive home with them. He would return clutching only one precious item, my mother's baby milk. Granny Eliza then had to hitch up her skirts and retrace his steps, picking up whatever she could find of his lost purchases.

This story should surely have been a clue as to what had been wrong with Charles; but it never occurred to me, and if Mum knew she never said. Quite simply, he was a drunkard. It is most likely that his Saturday evenings were spent at the Kangaroo Inn at Aston-on-Clun, which is about a mile south of Hopesay, and to which he would have walked along field footpaths. In the 1890's the publican at the Kangaroo was Richard Penney, who had been there for at least 30 years and had a son, similar in age to Charles, whom Charles would no doubt have known in boyhood. Before the Penneys ran the inn it had been run by Martha Teague, whose family also had links with the Pressdees – Martha and Elizabeth (Charles' grandmother) were close in age and both came from Diddlebury (a village about eight miles from Hopesay). Charles' father had a first, illegitimate, son (Jeremiah Pressdee Butler), and that son – Charles' elder brother – was a nurse-child at the inn in 1851. Household shopping could be done in Aston, and no doubt the Kangaroo provided a welcoming and familiar atmosphere before the trudge through the dark fields to the cottage in Perry Gutter. I guess that Charles probably regaled his fellow drinkers in the Kangaroo Inn and other drinking establishments with tales of his travels. In small villages and hamlets the village pub was the centre of social activity, where there might be newspapers (for those who could read), paraffin lamps, pub games, and company. For a man who had spent seven years in barracks with fellow soldiers, dark evenings in a cramped cottage with small children and his elderly mother-in-law for company would have been little competition for the fellowship and conviviality of the public house.

Both Charles and his younger brother Alfred had been in the army. Alfred had served in Gibraltar. Charles was sent to the East Indies after two years' service in the Royal Shropshire Regiment. Alfred's army record is unexceptional and undistinguished. He left as he had begun, a private, but without any black marks. His character is described as "temperate". Not so Charles.

Charles was almost twenty-three when he enlisted at Shrewsbury on 24th May 1877, joining the 21st Brigade of the 53rd (Shropshire) Regiment. This was a period when the army's recruitment of working men was changing and under review, for a variety of reasons. The 1870 Cardwell Reforms to the organisation and structure of the army had significantly reduced the minimum enlistment period and made the army more attractive to potential recruits, alongside less aggressive and more open recruitment practices. These, and other changes gradually improved the lot of soldiers. Between 1868 and 1880 numerous official bodies looked at army affairs, attempting to modernize the army and make it more efficient. Progress was slow, however, and conditions were still fairly poor, but recruiting increased in the last quarter of the nineteenth century. Agricultural depression and unemployment were key factors – the great agricultural depression of the latter part of the nineteenth century began in about 1875 and lasted for approximately twenty years. In 1878, almost one in four of the other ranks in the army were Irish, from, in the main, depressed rural areas and city slums. The army remained the last resort for men who could not get other work, and as well as economic casualties contained significant numbers of men who were deemed to be of "bad character" or on the edges of criminality. When Charles signed up, therefore, the army was still held in low esteem by most people, and Charles' family (who had been skilled craftsmen rather than labourers) may not have been best pleased with the life that he, and then Alfred, chose.

Charles served in the county until 4th March 1879 when he transferred to Aldershot. From there he proceeded immediately to Thayetmyo in Burma (arriving there on 28th April) where he remained for nearly four years. Thayetmyo was on the Irawaddy River, 200 miles north of Rangoon, with the fort just north of the town on the riverbank. In January 1881 he went to Bangalore, and in July that year was transferred to the newly formed 1st Battalion of the Oxfordshire Light Infantry. This regiment was formed as a consequence of the Childers reforms, which restructured the regiments of the army. The Oxfordshire Light Infantry began on 1st July 1881 – the day that Charles was transferred into it. On his return from India in 1884 Charles was briefly stationed in Oxford until his discharge. He was in the reserve for the next five years and his army service was fully completed in May 1889, less than one year before my mother's birth. While on the reserve he would have received fourpence a day from the army and was theoretically on recall for occasional training, although in general this did not take place. When Charles married in 1887 he was working as a labourer and might have been earning about £41 per year. The additional fourpence a day would have totalled over £6 per year, a significant boost to his earnings as employment conditions in Shropshire were particularly poor for labourers.

Throughout his service Charles remained a private. He was awarded the third class certificate of army education in October 1879 but did not progress further. For this certificate the soldier

18

had to be able to read aloud, take simple dictation, do basic arithmetic and understand simple accounts. The certificate was awarded on the recommendation of the Regimental schoolmaster. Men were generally only put forward for further study if they were deemed suitable for a future role as non-commissioned officers. Charles' army record appears to have been erratic. For instance, on 15th May 1882 he was granted extra pay for good conduct. This was withdrawn just two months later, and two years was deducted from his possible army pension. He would not have in fact qualified for a pension as his service was not long enough.

His character on discharge from the army reserve is given as "indifferent .. addicted to drink". Evidently it was not the army service my mother spoke of so proudly. During his time as a regular soldier he was treated for several illnesses by army doctors. While still in this country at the beginning of his service he was unfortunate enough to contract tonsilitis and was ill for ten days. Soon after his arrival in Burma he contracted diarrhoea, which was attributed by the army doctor to the climate and for which he spent six days in hospital, but subsequent bouts of dyspepsia are said to be of "uncertain" cause, or "constitutional". In 1881 he suffered from "general debility", said to be "constitutional" – and spent a month in hospital – but a wound for which he was treated in 1883 was due to a fall. However, we do not know of any ill health after he left the army during his early married life and in spite of surely not leading a healthy life in his later years, he lived until 1927, when he was seventy-four.

Life in the army for the ordinary soldier was tough, even after some of the reforms of the 1870's and 1880's. Stoppages for pay and payments for extra rations meant that it was not easy to save more than a few shillings a month, and the daily life consisted of frequent parades and often pointless guard duties, with little opportunities for recreation in barracks and an army uniform which was difficult to maintain and restrictive. Marriage was discouraged, venereal disease a major problem, medical treatment poor, and before discharge the ordinary soldier was not taught a skill or trade. Drinking and gambling were rife. In addition, it was felt that many of the recruits remained generally bad characters, and the army was held in low general regard (it was quite common for bars to have signs stating that soldiers were not admitted, and housemaids could be sacked for "walking out" with a soldier).

In extenuation of Charles, therefore, it can be said that he may well have acquired the drinking habit while in India. He must have been pretty uncomfortable there. In those days there was no hot weather uniform and soldiers wore the redcoat – made of wool – while on duty (the defeat of the British in the Zulu wars is partly attributed to this unsuitable costume). No doubt Charles became fond of India Pale Ale, which was brewed in Burton on Trent specifically for export to the British in India, including, of course, the army. Conditions in barracks in India may have improved somewhat by Charles' time, but were still likely to have been poor. Florence Nightingale had campaigned on this in the 1860's but in 1874 the Commander in Chief of the Army in India reported to her that "much needed improvements in army barracks were being delayed year after year."

Charles deserted his family and left two young children with a penniless old lady. My mother knew this and that it was the cause of her childhood having been spent in a workhouse orphanage. Yet she never spoke harshly of her father; in fact, I had always imagined him as someone like Hardy's Sergeant Troy in "Far From the Madding Crowd" – not exactly a good man, certainly, but a man of great charm and panache. Perhaps he was. We shall never know, because, of course, my mother never knew her father. But her granny and aunt must have withheld some of the truth when telling her about him, even though none of them had any reason to be grateful to him. I don't think now he really can have been like Sergeant Troy, though, like Uncle Alf, he might well have had some charm. I think I would have preferred to keep my illusions!

The description of Charles in his army records suggests that physically his son – my Uncle Alf – resembled him. Charles was 5'6" in height, weighing just over ten stone, with grey eyes, brown hair and "fresh" complexion. Alf also inherited something of his father's character I suspect, for Alf had a feckless streak, though he certainly did not desert his family. He didn't always pay his debts and I remember him once making his poor wife walk six miles back home late at night because after visiting our house he had an argument with one of the family. But he had great charm and we were all very fond of him. Alf is standing on the extreme left on the back row of my parents' wedding photograph.

It is hard to forgive Charles for abandoning his family, but I suspect his life consisted of attempts to escape what Melvin Bragg has called being "mired in Victorian rural poverty". He joined the army when it must have been clear to him that the village shoemaker would soon become a thing of the past, and that opportunities for work in the trade he had learnt were fast diminishing – the Victorian working class for the most part increasingly bought shoes made in the factories of Northampton, Leicestershire, and other centres. His mother had died and his family dispersed. At first he appeared to try to make a success of the army – the good conduct pay, and the army certificate of education – and his younger brother soon followed him into the army.

Drinking is another way of escaping but why Charles became a drunkard we shall never really know. We do know that agricultural wages for men were generally insufficient to support a family at this period without some additional earnings of women or older children in the family, so even without spending money on drink Charles would have found it difficult to support the old lady and the young children. His final unforgivable escape, by deserting his family, did not work out either, as we know from a brief encounter with Alf, much later, when Alf was a young man working for a time in North Wales as a farm labourer. One day an elderly man came to the farm, seeking casual work, or, possibly, begging. He addressed the young labourer, Alf, as "Sir". Alf was horrified when he realised that this was his father! He did not tell us what then happened, but this is the last anyone in my family heard of my grandfather. We have now discovered in our researches that he lived into his seventies and died in 1927 in Forden, Montgomeryshire, where he was still working as an agricultural labourer. The 1901 census shows that he was at that date at Stokesay, Shropshire, working as an agricultural labourer, and boarding with a local family, so it would seem that he moved around for work, and probably did not settle again for any length of time.

Chapter 4: Motherless, and now fatherless – who would look after Alf and Hilda?

It is easy to imagine Eliza's worry when Charles failed to return to the cottage in Perry Gutter. Was he lying on the field path, ill, dead, or, more likely, dead drunk? She must have left the children – then aged around five and one – with neighbours while she searched, and perhaps again when she subsequently sought help from the parish authorities in Hopesay. She was clearly a resourceful and, although uneducated, not inexperienced woman (in her youth she had travelled to London with her employer) but she had no income and was already in her sixties. She had lived in Perry Gutter for a long time and there were local families whom she would have known well, but there were no longer any of her family in the area to whom she could turn for support and assistance so she would have needed to ask for help from the parish clerk. This was James Dodd (born 1850 in Hopesay) whose father had been a shoemaker in Hopesay alongside Jeremiah Pressdee. James would have known Charles well, being only three years younger. James, too, had trained as a shoemaker but was now working as a gardener and had taken on the post of parish clerk, previously held by his father. He was supporting his wife and five children, one of whom was a daughter named Florence, born in the same year as Charles' daughter Florence (who had died). An older daughter was named Hilda. Whether or not the two men were friends, the parallels and differences in their lives – from very similar beginnings – would have been apparent, and may have made it harder for Charles to ask for help himself, or have intensified his temptation to leave. So it was left to Eliza to seek help, and answer questions about any possible support from other members of her family.

They must also have asked the old lady what she knew of her son-in-law's family. Presumably she had to say that he had little connection with them since leaving the army, and his only sibling in the area was his unmarried brother Alfred who had recently left the army reserve. The authorities would also have asked, I think, whether he was in receipt of an army pension (he wasn't). We do not know whether the authorities made any attempt to find him, or to make him pay towards his children's maintenance; if so, it was unsuccessful. The *Poor Law Unions Gazette* was published from 1857 to 1903 and consisted of detailed descriptions of "wanted" men who had deserted their families and left the union to take care of them. Of course, for all we know they might have contacted the army and decided from his record that it wouldn't be worth the trouble trying to locate him! So Mum's Auntie May, known to me for many years as my beloved Auntie Darwood, was contacted in Ladywood, Birmingham, where at that time she was living in a small terraced house with her husband, Mum's Uncle Ben, a glass cutter. We do not know how she was informed of what had happened, but I remember that years later when my father needed to be contacted because a bachelor uncle had met with a serious accident, a policeman came to our house. So it is possible that a policeman was sent to Auntie Darwood's house at 86 Morville Street, Ladywood, to break the news.

Ladywood is a suburb of inner city Birmingham, easily approached from one of the main routes out of the city, Broad Street, which houses the main Birmingham war memorial and many of the Council's offices, including the building where births and deaths are registered. In my childhood Ladywood had degenerated into a slum on its townward end, but further out, where it merged into Edgbaston, the houses were decent working class terraced houses, without yards or more houses behind them. In working class

24

Birmingham very poor housing was often built with two houses sharing the same rear wall and facing in opposite directions. These were "back to backs". In other cases the better houses lined the street, but an "entry" between two of them led to a yard, and another row of much smaller houses known as "back houses". These usually had a communal working area, as they were too small to accommodate a scullery, which the front houses included. Since the last war the area has been rebuilt, and now has blocks of high-rise flats.

Mum's aunt had worked as a servant in a public house before her marriage, first in Ludlow and later in Birmingham where she worked for her cousin Robert George Tedstone. This was at the Duke of Cambridge, in Great King Street. William Tedstone's brother Robert had migrated to Birmingham from Shropshire but the families clearly kept in touch as his son provided May (his cousin) with work and a home when she also moved to Birmingham. It is likely that this was how she met her husband, known to us as Uncle Ben, whom she had married in March 1886. I do not remember him, but my mother always told me that he was the kindest of men: whenever anyone in his wife's family was in trouble, he would say "Well, he (or she) will have to come here." Mum's older half-sister Kitty had already been taken in by the Darwoods and was living in their small house in Ladywood when Charles Pressdee deserted his family in Hopesay. In addition, by now there were two young sons – Will and Cecil – and May was either pregnant with, or more likely had already given birth to, her third child, Frank (born in July 1891). Thus, there were already six people (although four were children) in a home which only had three rooms.

May was later to have one more son, George, and three daughters, Dorothy, Ethel (who died in childhood) and Lucy, who was still a teenager when I first knew them. By then, however, the family had migrated to a larger house (although they remained in the three roomed house until at least 1904). Their later home was also in Ladywood – 106 Rann Street, a corner house, with many facilities that her first home lacked. Although old-fashioned and with an outside toilet, it had several bedrooms, a large attic, a good-sized walk-in pantry, two "parlours" or sitting rooms, and a decent kitchen and scullery. But, earlier, when she learned of the distress Charles had left her mother to cope with, it would have been impossible to take any more young children into her small home. She would not leave her mother, however, to have to end her days in the workhouse. So, difficult though it must have been, the old lady went to live with the Darwood family.

How Eliza made the journey to Birmingham, involving as it did two changes of train, is not known. It would be a reasonable guess, and in character, if Ben Darwood had fetched her. It seems unlikely that an illiterate and largely penniless old lady would have been able to make a long railway journey involving several changes unaccompanied. In an interview with a reporter from the *Birmingham Gazette* in 1917 Eliza described going to Craven Arms in April 1852 when her son George was a baby to see the first train there, and the celebrations, but she said that "a good many were afraid to ride. I myself was a long time before I rode in a train." Assuming that Ben had gone to fetch her, the first part of their journey would have either been on foot, or possibly by carrier's cart to Craven Arms railway station, from where they would have taken a train to Shrewsbury. From the imposing Victorian Gothic station of Shrewsbury, their next train would have taken them to Birmingham Snow Hill station via Wellington,

Shifnal and Wolverhampton Low Level. The Snow Hill station, where they disembarked, would have been quite different from the 1906 GWR terminus, which is still remembered by many people living in the West Midlands area. The original station would have been a smaller, more cramped structure with a vaulted roof.

When Mum was born in 1890 the word "orphan" was used for anyone who had lost one parent. So for Mum and Uncle Alf, there being no-one in the family who could look after them, there was no alternative but to go into the orphans' section of the nearest workhouse. They were therefore, as we would term it today, "taken into care". With most of their immediate relatives now in the city of Birmingham, the two children remained in Shropshire.

Chapter 5: The city and the country

One of the main cradles of the industrial revolution in the eighteenth century was central Shropshire, the area of Coalbrookdale close to where the first all-iron bridge crosses the River Severn. Here the large-scale commercial production of cast iron products first took place and by the time Hilda was born, the whole area north of the Severn where the modern town of Telford is now situated had become a thriving industrial area. The main industries were iron founding, engineering, clay products and terracotta production, and coal mining extended down the Severn Valley almost as far as Bewdley. However, the area of southwest Shropshire where Hilda lived was completely untouched by any industry, and was, as it still is, deeply rural.

In 1848 Marx described the changes taking place with traditional social structures being replaced as industrialisation spread. These changes continued during my mother's childhood. Old country crafts were disappearing, as exemplified by my grandfather's original training in the shoe trade. The tranter (a peddler, typically hiring himself out with his horse and cart) in Hardy's "Under the Greenwood Tree" is another example of a village trade which would not survive. Towns were growing apace and country people were migrating to them and many were becoming factory workers.

Birmingham, known as the "city of a thousand trades", was already large when my mother was born, and was still growing. At the beginning of the nineteenth century, Birmingham had a population of about 74,000. By the end of the century it had grown to 750,000. This rapid population growth meant that by the middle of the century Birmingham had become the second largest population centre in Britain.

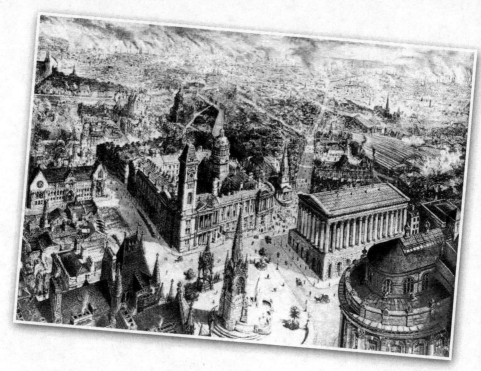

*An old drawing of Birmingham city centre
in 1886, looking over Chamberlain Square,
with its civic buildings and Chamberlain Memorial.*

By the end of that century Birmingham had two mainline railway
stations, an imposing town hall, museum and art gallery, and
Mason College (the nucleus of Birmingham University, which was
founded in 1900). The Gothic façade of King Edward's School
occupied much of the main street, and in 1880 one of the first
girls' grammar schools to be established was added at right angles
to the boys' school. Joseph Chamberlain had become the city's
mayor in 1873 and was responsible for much of the city centre
development, including libraries, municipal swimming pools and
concert halls. Armaments had been produced in Birmingham

since the seventeenth century, when the city had helped to arm Cromwell, and brass production and product manufacture were key industries. The city was also the home of Cadbury's chocolate, and numerous other factories of all kinds, many of them quite small. By the end of the nineteenth century there were approximately 2000 factory chimneys in the Birmingham area. When Eliza went to live there it was a vibrant, thriving place with large stores, electric trams and impressive municipal buildings. And since 1889 Birmingham had officially been a "city".

Birmingham and its neighbouring industrial areas attracted many people from the surrounding counties, including Shropshire. Our researches show that most of Hilda's closest relatives had moved to the towns – uncles, aunts, great-uncles and cousins – and then often assisted the next generation of family migrants with work and accommodation. Even Charles' father Jeremiah, the shoemaker, ended his life as a foreman at a chemical works in Dudley, working for one of his nephews. While the population of England and Wales doubled from 1851 to 1911, in rural areas the net population increase was only 13%, as people migrated to the towns. There was not an absolute divide between the rural areas and towns: some agricultural workers lived in towns, and people from agricultural families maintained links with their families in the country, as was the case in Hilda's family. There were similar links for my father's family. His parents had both been born in Birmingham but all four of his grandparents were from country areas (Worcestershire and Warwickshire). One grandfather became a railway worker having previously been an agricultural labourer, and the other was an agricultural labourer, then a carter, and then a coal merchant. I remember going on a trip to the country when I was quite a young child to see relatives of my grandmother's (I think they must have been cousins) who lived in a small cottage.

As many city dwellers were recent migrants from the country –
with a significant number returning there for seasonal work – and
with industrial workers increasingly populating rural areas as
railways and other industries spread (albeit often on a temporary
basis), urban and rural worlds remained closely connected.

However, as the city populations expanded during the nineteenth
century, some people fell on hard times. Unemployment, sickness,
age, all took their toll in both towns and country. Earlier in the
nineteenth century such unfortunates could obtain outdoor relief
while living in their own homes: the small parish homes, or
workhouses, which existed were not normally feared or hated by
the local community. People who lived in small towns and villages
knew one another and the scale of relief was human, even friendly,
although it could be harsh. The Old Poor Law provided a wide
range of support, including unemployment relief, and payments
for items such as food, clothing, rent, fuel and furniture. It could
cover doctors' bills and the cost of nursing. The generosity of the
parishes varied, with the north and west generally harsher than the
south and east parts of the country, but many rural workers
received poor law assistance at some stage in their lives, with
estimates of at least half of rural families receiving help
occasionally in their lives, and at least a third receiving help on a
regular basis. As Marx pointed out, all this changed as the
economics and ethos of the capitalist system took over in Britain.
As the cities expanded, a new and harsher structure of relief
became necessary, and this was imposed upon both city and
country alike.

Chapter 6: The workhouse in Bishops Castle

In 1834 a new Poor Law was enacted. A central authority, called the Poor Law Commission, was set up with three major Commissioners, and others working under them. In 1847 this became the Poor Law Board, and after 1871 the Poor Law was administered by local government Boards. To save money, parishes were grouped together into "Unions", each of which would be run by a local committee of Guardians, elected by rate-payers, responsible to the Board.

Under the new law, accommodation was to be provided for "paupers" in workhouses. It was stipulated that this was to be "worse" than the normal living conditions of the poorest labourer – a deterrent which no doubt contributed to the fear and loathing in which these institutions were originally held, well illustrated by Dickens in *Oliver Twist*. The 1834 Act also abolished "outdoor relief" to "the able-bodied". Thus, people in need had no alternative to the workhouse and in the middle years of the nineteenth century many new ones were built, including the workhouse in Bishops Castle.

The Clun Poor Law Union was established on 13 July 1836, and comprised a number of parishes to the South and North of Clun. Most of these were in villages and hamlets, but three main centres were included: Clun, Bishops Castle, and Lydbury North. Both Clun and Bishops Castle had small, old poorhouses, which were in use. These were acquired by the newly formed Union. There was some difficulty over the acquisition of the poorhouse in Clun as the owner, one Philip Morris, was clearly afraid of possible loss of money when the building was compulsorily acquired. He tried to forestall this by selling it to the Union. The sale was actually invalid, as Morris was really only a trustee, and not the legal owner, whose identity is not known. Whether Morris succeeded in acquiring any money is not recorded; if he did, he managed to swindle the union officers.

This was not the end of the problems, because the Clun Guardians would not agree that a new building should be erected. They continued to use the old malthouse in Clun, which had been the poorhouse, in conjunction with a building in Bishops Castle which housed "pauper" children (as workhouse inmates were always designated). It was not until later in 1840 that Bishops Castle was chosen as the site because it was the most central of the three towns in the Union. Today the workhouse is no more, with only one boundary wall remaining. It is, however, remembered in the name of Union Street.

The site at Potters Close was to cost no more than £400, and the maximum expenditure on the building was to be £2600. These figures were too much for the Guardians, who tried to back out yet again, producing plans the following year to improve the Clun poorhouse at a cost of £90, although they agreed to spend a further £150 on improvements at Bishops Castle, stating that the majority of the Guardians were determined to "resist all further expense".

The Assistant Commissioner William Day was able to veto this inadequate proposal and to insist that the plan should be accepted. He was appointed to oversee the building of the workhouse. He appears to have been tactful and long-suffering in his dealings with those responsible for the work of the Union. In a statement written at the commencement of the negotiations, he wrote: "The union is generally of an unsatisfactory character ..... the Guardians are farmers and shopkeepers of a very inferior grade ..... totally unable to weigh the advantages of principle against an apparently immediate expense". He added that he thought they "act from ignorance and timidity rather than from ill will". No doubt Day was an educated man himself, and he seems to have wanted to do the best he could for the "paupers" who were to be the inmates of the workhouse. His comments do not lack generosity. At all events, he managed to obtain the consent of the Poor Law Commission and to get an architect appointed and his design approved by 25th August 1842.

Photograph: Clun Union Workhouse, Union St., Bishop's Castle, 1904 © SWSHAS from Mr. Ian Henderson, grandson of Frank Leonard Davies, Master of Workhouse

The architect was Henry John Whiting, who practised in Shrewsbury. He had already designed workhouses in Dorset and in Rhayader in Radnorshire. The latter place was to become famous as the source of Birmingham's water. The design of the Clun workhouse was cruciform style and would accommodate up to one hundred and fifty paupers, and staff. It contained a central block, which housed the master and matron, four airing yards (for the separate use of boys, girls, men and women), and across the middle of the building, the arms of the crucifix, the left being for females and the right for males. This was a conventional design and although the original idea had been to incorporate a hospital area, this was omitted, as was a water closet, soil pits being substituted for privies. This was later improved. The two-storied building contained a dining area, a lying-in room, a laundry, together with dormitory accommodation for boys, girls, men, and women – all designated "paupers". The sexes were separated without regard for their relationships: Mum would have been, in the main, kept apart from my Uncle Alf. No great hardship for her, as she was only about one or two years old when they went there, but he, aged five, must have missed his baby sister.

The architect made considerable specifications for windows and for the pitch of roofs, which were to be higher at the front of the building than at the back, and included parapets, porches and gable ends, all of which were omitted and replaced by cheaper utilitarian arrangements with barge boards on projecting edges. The building was stone built, and in December 1904 was officially named "Stone House", a name it still had when, in later years, it was used for a time as a hospital.

The building contained a Church of England chapel. Sunday attendance at services was compulsory, but over time the rules were amended to allow for other faiths or denominations to be recognised. There does not seem to have been an option for agnostics or atheists, but no doubt those who did not want to attend the services would suddenly have been converted to one of these named denominations! My mother owned a bible and a prayer book, still in my possession, which I used to believe were Sunday school prizes. They were actually prizes she received from the all-age elementary school she attended. The bible is the revised version and is inscribed "Bishops Castle Elementary School, Wright's Charity, Prize for Classwork, awarded to Hilda Pressdee, Standard 7, 1904." It was printed "On behalf of the British and Foreign Bible Society" by the Cambridge University Press, 1900. Wright's Charity gave books to primary school pupils (operating from about the mid-nineteenth century until the early years of this century). There had been a Wright's Charity School in Bishops Castle, although its exact dates and site are not clear. The prayer book is inscribed "Hilda Pressdee from Rev. P. Thomas March 18 1900".

The architect included considerable embellishment in his original plans, only some of which were actually made. For instance, the windows were supposed to have oak frames, and decorative quarry glazing with leaded edging, but they became simple iron casements. However, some decoration remained: the front entrance doors to the building had fancy hinges, and Gothic decoration above them, and the Guardians' Board Room (for they met in the workhouse) had panelled doors with Gothic heads. The chapel windows also received some embellishment, although not stained glass.

The workhouse was built by the firm of Joseph Menhennitt, of Radnor, which appears to have been paid in instalments. However, with this gentleman too the Guardians fell into dispute, and in

1845 there is an instruction to the clerk to institute proceedings to recover a balance due from him. It is not clear whether Menhennitt had been overpaid, or, more probably, had failed to complete the work for which he had been paid.

Further problems arose when the architect, who was, of course, supposed to ensure that the building was properly built, fled the country in order to evade his considerable number of debtors! The new architect, a Mr Haycock, made some alteration to the plans, adding two small yards for male and female vagrants, two special punishment wards, and – surely an omission in the original plans – a "dead house", i.e. a mortuary. It was after all, to be expected that deaths would occur from time to time. All this made it necessary for the Guardians to apply to the public works commission for a loan of £1500, which they agreed to repay over a period of ten years.

The workhouse opened in 1845 but the troubles of the Guardians were not over. A relieving officer in their employ was found to have been trading as a fishmonger and illegally employing paupers as cheap labour. In 1846 the Guardians appointed as workhouse master one Francis Williams, who was discovered to be incompetent. Among other things he did not know how to keep his accounts. They were preparing to dismiss him, but he resigned to avoid this, and a little later was found dead in his bed, having cut his throat. The coroner's verdict was that he had committed suicide "in a fit of insanity". This unfortunate man does not appear to have been the only one who might have been thought to be incompetent!

Chapter 7: Mum's life in the workhouse

Admission to a workhouse was always voluntary. Mum was classed as an orphan but her aunt may have been regarded as her guardian. We do not know whether Auntie Darwood made the request for the children to enter the workhouse; if she did, it would have been with deep regret. This hard working and loving woman clearly wanted to do what she could for her dead sister's children and in later years my mother always referred to her aunt's house as "home". This actually annoyed my father: I think he found it hurtful because he had clearly provided a pleasant home for his wife and children, and coming from an emotionally secure background there was much he never really understood about his wife.

We do not know the exact date when Hilda and Alf went into the workhouse, but it was while Hilda was still a baby, certainly not more than two years old. She would not have been old enough to live in the children's section of the workhouse, and might have been looked after by a woman inmate. There are no records about this, though sometimes a nurse was employed in the workhouse for such work.

Hilda would have been transferred to the girls' section by the age of three or four. The names of inmates in the workhouse at this period have not been preserved other than on census records, and apart from three much later specific references to my mother, the only record we have of Hilda's life in the workhouse is the entry in the census of 1901. Here she is shown as one of thirteen girls living in the workhouse, all aged between seven and thirteen, except for two younger children whose parents were also inmates. Boys of that age are all designated "scholar". However, no occupation is given for the girls, although they all attended the same school! The ages may be inaccurate, as my mother is recorded as aged nine; in fact, she was a few days short of eleven. It is interesting to note that there were only nineteen children in the Clun workhouse in 1901 (this included five groups of siblings). At earlier periods there had been more children – in 1861 there were thirty-five, in 1871 forty and in 1881 thirty. By 1891, however, numbers had reduced and there were only fourteen (of whom eight appeared to have parents also in the workhouse). Towards the end of the nineteenth century, poor law unions moved towards boarding out pauper children in the parish, so this may account for the lower numbers of children shown as resident in the Bishops Castle workhouse when the later censuses were taken. The fact that there were no children under the age of 6 in the workhouse in 1901 other than two who were with their parents also seems to confirm this. Hilda appears to have been one of the last group of very young children who were brought up in the workhouse.

In the Guardians' reports, largely financial, my mother is, however, mentioned three times. The first of these reads: "Hilda Pressdee, an indoor pauper. The clerk read a letter from Mrs Darwood of Birmingham applying for permission for this pauper, her niece, to visit her for a fortnight's holiday. It was unanimously resolved that the pauper be allowed to go, if the aunt pay her travelling expenses and make suitable arrangements for the journey." This was dated 7th August 1902, when Hilda was now twelve. Her brother Alf would already have left the workhouse. Auntie Darwood did make the required arrangements for the visit, though she was fairly poor at that time: she had a growing family, one of her children was a scholarship boy at George Dixon Grammar School, and she took in washing to supplement her husband's wages.

We have no information on Mum's journey, but it seems likely that she went alone, as at the age if twelve she was probably thought able to do this, following instructions. The first part of this journey, which would have involved three changes, would have been over the Bishop's Castle Railway. This ramshackle and overgrown line ran for ten and a half miles down to Stretford Bridge Junction on the Shrewsbury to Chester line, just outside Craven Arms. In the early 1860s there was a plan to build a railway from Craven Arms to Montgomery with a branch line from Lydham to Bishops Castle. The money ran out halfway through construction, causing a dead end at Lydham with trains having to reverse direction to reach Bishops Castle. And shortly after opening, in 1867 the company went into receivership in which it remained for the whole of its sixty-nine year life. There were intermediate stations at Stretford Bridge, Plowden, Eaton and Lydham Heath. Although it never made any money, the railway nevertheless played an important role in the commercial life of Bishops Castle, struggling on with second-hand rolling stock until its closure in 1935. Today all that remains is a small railway museum in the town.

In 1903 Mum again spent a fortnight's holiday in her aunt's home, and on 6th May 1904, when Mum was fourteen years old, it was unanimously agreed that "this child" (no longer designated pauper) be released into the care of her aunt, of 86 Morville Street, Birmingham, at the end of June. Again, the railway fare was to be paid by her aunt, even though Hilda was now leaving to take up employment arranged by the penny-pinching Guardians. However, the Guardians were actually going to provide my mother with new clothes; she would leave the workhouse forever wearing "the usual outfit for a child going into service". This tells us two things: first, that girls from the workhouse were usually placed in service, and secondly, that her normal clothes were no longer suitable. This is because until this time Mum would have worn workhouse uniform, though we do not know what this was like. There are records from other workhouses up and down the country that there was an industry providing workhouse uniforms made of coarse material, and there exists a photograph of two old men walking in the main street of Bishops Castle wearing workhouse uniform. Workhouse girls also usually had their hair cropped short (because of problems with lice in their sleeping quarters) and would thus have been clearly identifiable as workhouse inmates wherever they went. The more humane workhouses allowed the girls to grow their hair before they went out into service, so when Mum left in 1904 she may have been enabled to feel that she was less obviously from a workhouse. This would not have been the case, however, in her earlier visits to Auntie Darwood, although knowing my aunt's nature I imagine she would have had some other clothes ready for Mum to wear during her stay (even if she had to borrow them).

I do not know whether my mother suffered any of the diseases of childhood, but, as I remember, she had two vaccination marks. Vaccination for smallpox was compulsory and remained so for many more years (Charles' army records show that he had already been vaccinated before signing up). The workhouse regime provided three meals a day and nothing in between. By the time Mum was living in the workhouse these were quite appetizing and nutritious, and she grew up to be very strong and active, as I remember her, and she was rarely ill. In 1901 a Manual of Workhouse Cookery was prepared by the National Training School of Cookery and issued to Boards of Guardians by the Local Government Board. It contains basic rules of the various kinds of cooking and many recipes including meat, fish and several puddings. Anyone experiencing this diet would certainly have been better fed than the majority of working people at this time and it is likely that Mum's diet throughout her time in the workhouse was far superior to that which she would have received had she been brought up in Perry Gutter. If you were unemployed in those days you went without. When my sister and I turned our noses up at a meal my mother used to tell us that our father had once had to eat herrings for his Christmas Day meal. Whether this was apocryphal I don't know, but it served as a timely threat!

But life in the workhouse when she was first there must still have been pretty grim for a young child. From 1891 unions could buy toys for the workhouses, so hopefully there were some toys for Mum to play with as she grew up (perhaps paid for out of charitable monies or provided by local benefactors if the local Guardians were not prepared to meet this expense?) There are no records from the Bishops Castle workhouse specifically, but in other areas in the early twentieth century Christmas Day was celebrated in the workhouse. However, in the early days of workhouses Christmas Day was commonly not celebrated, and my mother never mentioned Christmas celebrations in her childhood. Our family Christmas celebrations were, I think, copied from my father's family traditions. Whether Mum ever received any presents as a child I do not know. Newspaper reports show that in 1901 there was a subscription New Year's Dinner at the workhouse, with a large Christmas tree from which all the inmates were given a small gift, and a generous dinner served. At the same time, the owner of the Three Tuns (a well-known Bishops Castle pub) proposed inviting the inmates to an afternoon performance by a choir, but the Guardians refused to allow anyone to go. So inmates were clearly allowed only a certain amount of enjoyment. Mum almost certainly never had birthday presents – she only knew that her birthday was in early April. In later life her husband and children always celebrated it on April 1st and it was only when Mum reached pension age and records were checked that it was discovered that her birthday was actually April 12th.

The girls all slept in a dormitory on the left of the building. The single beds were wooden but need not have been uncomfortable. However, the behaviour of one sad little girl raises another question – punishments. Which child of those listed in the census return this was I do not know, but one girl was a bed-wetter. Mum told me that this poor girl, having been punished for the offence, decided to avoid further punishment by implicating everyone else. She carefully and systematically wet all the beds in the dormitory. Boys were frequently beaten in workhouses but workhouse girls could not legally be treated in this way, although it is clear that this little girl dreaded being punished again, whatever form that took.

School attendance had been compulsory since the Forster Act of 1870. The school leaving age had gradually been raised since then: in 1880 attendance became compulsory for children between the ages of five and ten, and in 1893 the school leaving age was raised to 12. In my mother's day it was fourteen, and remained so until the wartime act of 1944, which began the process of raising it until it became what it is now, sixteen. In fact the exact age at which a child ceased to attend school depended on his or her birthday. My father left school at thirteen as his birthday was during the school holidays in August. Mum left school a few months after her fourteenth birthday at the end of the summer term in 1904. Many larger workhouses included a school and a schoolmaster was appointed in Bishops Castle when the workhouse first opened, but there is no record of any teaching being done there.

*The old school building
at Bishop's Castle*

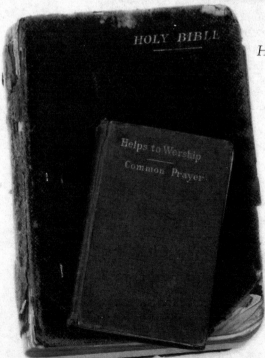

Hilda's prizes

The Bishops Castle workhouse children attended the town's all-age elementary school. It had been built in 1845. The Forster Act permitted school boards to provide schools where voluntary schools were inadequate: this was not required in Bishops Castle. The school could accept 170 children, though attendance never averaged more than 128. There was an endowment of £16 a year originally, though this would not have covered the expenses. The building is still there; however the inside of the building has been gutted and it is now a large chemist's store. On the front of the building the entrance marked "Boys and Girls" remains. Originally the school had three teachers: a master, a mistress, and an infants' teacher. The school was also the first telegraph office in the town!

Mum did well at school. She received three school prizes: a Bible, a Prayer Book, and a novel called *Daisy*. I still have the first two, but *Daisy* has disappeared. I read it when I was a child and remember it as a tale about a slave plantation in the Deep South of America, so it must have been written by someone who opposed slavery, but I have not been able to trace this novel. From the way my mother used to speak to us about her schooldays I think she must have enjoyed her school life. I remember that she used to recite to us Tennyson's poem about a dying child who had hoped to be "Queen of the May". I don't think the old custom of electing a May Queen was practised in Bishops Castle at this time, but Mum seemed to know about it. There is an account of May Day celebrations in Hardy's *Tess of the D'Urbervilles*. And in Aston on Clun, where Charles frequented the Kangaroo Pub, there were, and still continue, festivities on the last Sunday in each May – Arbor Day – when a poplar tree is bedecked with flags. Mum's family would have been familiar with this local tradition, and no doubt told her about it in later years.

My father left school at the age of thirteen, but, in Birmingham, was able to extend his education at night school. I still have his complete Shakespeare, which was an evening school prize. Night school would not have been an option in rural Shropshire. Literacy among working people in the towns was greater than is often supposed. My paternal grandmother, who was born in 1854, was an avid reader who used to give me books, and working class people who joined the developing Trade Union movement and socialist organisations created by Hyndman and Morris were certainly literate. Literacy levels usually lagged behind in rural areas, however, where not all agricultural workers placed a high value on schooling. But both Mum's parents were literate, as were her grandfathers, so it seems that her family did value education.

Mum's walk from the workhouse to the school would have taken only a few minutes, and the children seem not to have been supervised. She told me that girls and boys went together and often managed to "dilly dally on the way". She remembered some of the pranks the boys got up to. One in particular was unpleasant, for they sometimes used to catch small birds, such as sparrows or blue tits, cut off their heads (or perhaps more cruelly pull them off) and then watch the headless birds appear to dance, from the twitching of the dying creatures' limbs.

It may have been on the way to or from school that Mum saw some of the peddlers and other itinerants. Bishops Castle was a market town, with drovers bringing sheep and cattle – often from some distance – so at market and fair times would have had its population considerably swelled by traders and visitors. One itinerant who visited the town Mum never forgot and often described to her children. He arrived leading a brown bear. The man had some sort of musical instrument – Mum never said what, but it may have been a fiddle. The bear was tied to a pole and when the man played some music, the bear danced. It must have been an unforgettable sight.

An account of the celebrations for Queen Victoria's Diamond Jubilee on June 22nd 1897 by a twelve-year-old girl in Lydbury North (about three miles from Bishops Castle) describes the local celebrations, including rosettes, a decorated schoolroom, games, races, singing, tea and sweets. The girls were given brooches, and the boys medals (*South West Shropshire Historical and Archaeological Society Journal*, Summer 1998). Hilda would have been seven years old at that time – the workhouse children were likely to have participated in similar activities organised in Bishops Castle. In the latter part of the nineteenth century workhouse children were often included in treats and outings organised by the local community, which was generally sympathetic to these children. The children would, nevertheless, have been very conscious of the gap between them and the community beyond the workhouse. This may have been slightly less so in towns where, as in Bishops Castle, the workhouse children went to the local school, but must still have been very marked when, at the end of school, most children went back to their family homes and the workhouse children, in their uniforms, walked together back to the workhouse.

Mum knew how to escape from the workhouse, however, when she wanted to. She told me that she used to jump out of a window and land on the potato "tump". She didn't appear to have been punished for this. I had always thought she meant "dump" but when I was talking to a local woman in Bishops Castle she instantly knew that the correct word was "tump". This is actually a local dialect word for a mound (an "unty tump" is a mole hill!) Potatoes were stored for the winter in a large pile and covered with soil. This suggests that the adults who stayed in the other end of the workhouse may well have been working in the grounds and cultivating vegetables.

Though the regime in the workhouse was strict, and many things that most children take for granted – favourite toys, picture books, a bedtime story – Mum did not remember, she never made me think that she had been unhappy in the workhouse. Mum entered the workhouse as a pauper; when she left it she had become "a child". Does this indicate a change in the attitude of the authorities to those in their charge? I think it might. They had, after all, become good enough Christians to share Christmas with workhouse children. Whether this extended to the vagrants, the old, the crippled and the lunatics who occupied the other part of the workhouse is probably doubtful. Moreover, abuse was widespread. During my mother's time in the workhouse there was one Master who sexually abused some of the girl inmates, including my mother, something she only told one of her sons towards the end of her life. When she went on her third journey to Birmingham in 1904 at the age of fourteen, with new clothes and a new life ahead of her, she must have felt excited and relieved, and glad that this time she did not have a return ticket.

Chapter 8: Adults in the workhouse

Responsibility for the day-to-day running of the workhouse rested with a married couple known as "The Master and Mistress". Because the Bishops Castle workhouse was relatively small, the master and mistress did not remain in their post for very long. People who undertook this job made it their career, typically starting in a small workhouse and then moving on to a larger one, where the wages were correspondingly higher. During Mum's time in the Bishops Castle workhouse there were nine different Masters.

The workhouse had two basic sections; the orphanage, and, on the other side of the building, adults in need were housed. These included old people who could no longer work, and were therefore destitute, short stay vagrants, and lunatics. The able-bodied were required to work for their keep: women helped with cleaning or caring for babies; men, were required to maintain the building and work in the grounds. The 1901 census record for the Bishops Castle workhouse lists 23 men inmates, of whom all but 5 were elderly, and 8 women inmates, of whom 4 were elderly. In 1901 a report in the local paper was critical of staffing levels at the workhouse, due to the fact that there were fewer able-bodied inmates to assist.

Mum told us very little about the adult section of the workhouse, and I do not think she saw much of the adult inmates. If, as seems likely, she saw the queues of vagrants in the street waiting for admittance, she never mentioned this to us. There was, however, one nine day wonder, which she told us about: one old woman who had lost her reason managed to escape. She was naked, and ran into a nearby wood where she climbed a tree. Mum said the police had to be summoned to bring her back – another sad tale of those times. I used to imagine this woman hiding in the tree and can still summon up this picture – Mum must have recounted it vividly. It was to be many years before the treatment of people with mental disorders improved.

The workhouses officially closed in 1930, but the Trade Union leader Jack Jones recalled that in 1934 the unemployed who took part in what became known as the Hunger Marches were sometimes put up overnight in the empty workhouse buildings, and that they slept on bare boards and were each provided with one blanket, after receiving some hunks of bread and cheese. He believed that this was probably fairly similar to what had been the normal treatment of homeless vagrants when they turned up at workhouses.

Chapter 9: Hilda's life after the workhouse, and then marriage

Like virtually all girls leaving workhouses, Mum's destination was a job as a live-in servant. This was also the main occupation at that time for girls from rural families, and all her close female relatives had worked as servants, at private houses or in pubs. Had she been brought up in Perry Gutter, her destination – service, and the city – would probably have been the same. Mum told me that her first job was as a maid of all work with a German family then living in Birmingham. That it was in Birmingham makes me think that either Auntie Darwood arranged it, or that the workhouse was asked to arrange a post there if possible. Mum laughed when she told me that during the First World War, when all German people who lived in England were suspected of being spies, she used to wonder whether she had worked for spies! She did not remain for long in the private service post that had been found for her. She chose to find work in hospital kitchens. At one stage she worked for a Birmingham hospital, and the 1911 census shows that she was by then working as a live-in kitchen maid at the Rochdale Infirmary. The new Rochdale Infirmary had been opened in 1883, so when Mum worked there it would still have been reasonably modern.

She was, however, young and inexperienced, probably still very much a country girl. At the age of twenty-three she became pregnant, and my half-brother Ralph was born a little before her twenty fourth birthday, on 13th February 1914. The birth took place in Leeds at 22 Brunswick Place, which appears to have been a mother and baby home for unmarried mothers, but the address Mum gave on Ralph's birth certificate is that of Auntie Darwood in Birmingham – she had clearly left or been asked to leave wherever she had previously been working in Leeds. We don't know much about her circumstances then, but she did describe how, without help and desperate, she spent her last pennies on soap to keep the baby clean. She also told me that the nuns at a convent near to Bury, in Lancashire, gave her shelter. This was Holly Mount in Tottington, where a convent ran a children's home. It was established in 1888 when it was becoming common for local Boards of Guardians to place children with Catholic Rescue Homes (who tended to charge lower rates for children whom they took in). Holly Mount looked after girls, and presumably babies. A home run by monks in Rochdale (Buckley Hall) provided care for boys.

Eventually Ralph was boarded with a pleasant couple who lived in Rochdale. Mr and Mrs Butterworth looked after Ralph until 1923, when Mum, now married, at last had a home of her own. My paternal grandfather died in 1922 and at some point in the following year my grandmother and my uncle Fred moved back to what had been her parents' home at 158 Windsor Street, Aston, to live with her unmarried brother Jack. This move gave my parents enough space for their family (I was born in 1920 and my sister in 1923) and also for Ralph to join us. Mum took me with her to fetch him and I can just remember walking between railway stations in Manchester, Ralph pushing his wheelbarrow filled with all his toys. As a young man he joined the army and then served throughout the Second World War. He married, had four children, and died at the age of sixty-eight. In later years he and my father used to go on holidays together, Ralph driving in the old veteran cars he liked.

We do not know when Mum returned to Birmingham, but it was probably just a few months after Ralph's birth as she was living in Birmingham with Auntie Darwood during the First World War.

Assuming she was in Lancashire for a little longer, it may have been the outbreak of war and opportunity for work which provided a suitable reason for a return to Birmingham. How she must have felt, leaving her small child in care in Lancashire, we can only imagine. I am fairly certain from subsequent events that she did not tell her Aunt about the baby, although she would have told my father before they married. Mum's closest female relatives on her mother's side in Shropshire – her own mother, her grandmother Eliza, her two aunts – all had illegitimate children who were raised in the family home, with the exception of Auntie Darwood (although it is clear that when she married Uncle Ben she was already expecting her first child). But Mum is unlikely to have known a lot about her family history, and attitudes in the city towards illegitimacy were very different from attitudes in the country. While Auntie Darwood was very accepting of Ralph once she knew about him, it was some time before my mother managed to tell her. She had, after all, initially kept his birth a secret from the family.

Mum's older sister Kitty (who had been brought up by Auntie Darwood after Sarah's death) also had an illegitimate child, Donald, who was born in June 1912 in Yorkshire where she had been working as a nurse. Later, Kitty lived at the Darwoods' home too (although she worked away from there for significant periods) and Donald's home was with Auntie Darwood. So whether Kitty and Donald were already at Auntie Darwood's when Mum arrived back there we do not know. At any rate the home, although having six rooms plus the kitchen, was getting fairly crowded again at this point since the Darwoods still had six children living at home (of whom the four eldest – all sons – were adults) and the old lady Eliza.

Mum worked, as she termed it, "on munitions". As the war dragged on it became necessary for women to undertake many tasks previously performed only by men; men now in the trenches, or dead or wounded. Arms and ammunition now became needed in great quantities. In 1915 Lloyd George became Minister of Munitions and took control of factories producing arms of all kinds. Some writers comment that women volunteered to work in munition factories for patriotic reasons. This may have been true for some of them, particularly those with middle class backgrounds, who certainly worked loyally in the factories, but many poorer women (both single and married) must have been attracted by the high wages that were now available to them. This must have been the case with my mother. While doing munitions work she was living in a home where at least two of her cousins were conscientious objectors and served prison sentences for refusing to accept orders because of their socialist opposition to the war. It was a household that was opposed to the war, but also a working class home, which needed work. Mum also had Ralph to support. I would therefore be very surprised if she volunteered to work "on munitions" as she termed it, for patriotic reasons. In 1916 a triangular metal brooch was issued to women working in munitions factories – the 'War Service' badge (many of which were actually made in Birmingham). If my mother wore this (it apparently helped women to get seats on buses!) it would probably have been for practical rather than patriotic reasons. The lifelong friend whom Mum first met while doing this work – who later became my Auntie Lily – had spent her youth in such hardship and poverty that for her, too, the chance to earn good money in the munitions factory must have seemed like a golden opportunity.

However, in 1915 Lloyd George had to meet widespread opposition to the recruitment of women, even though the

Suffragette movement supported him. Some of the opposition came from the Trade Union movement, largely because men were afraid women might steal some of their jobs. In munitions factories, the "Munitionettes", as they came to be called, were of all ages although the majority were young women under thirty-five. By Armistice Day 950,000 women were working in munitions. They came from all parts of the British Isles, rather surprisingly, perhaps, including Ireland. Most of the newer munition factories staffed wholly by women were in Southern England but in other areas existing industries expanded and employed women. Birmingham was one of the particularly large munition centres. From 1917 women had to receive training before they could work in munitions but before that training was on the job, and this is probably how my mother was taught. The women did a variety of jobs, including some work which must have required training, such as gear cutting, riveting and crane driving, but the majority (which I think included my mother) spent their time filling and packing shells and bullets. This was dangerous work which took place in what became known as "danger buildings" – dangerous, because these areas could easily have been ignited.

The buildings themselves were often old and dilapidated, especially in the Birmingham factories. The work was also unhealthy, often causing headaches and sore throats, and the hands of the women who handled gunpowder became stained yellow. As a result they were often called, jokingly, "canaries". The overseers were usually drawn from the better-educated women from the middle classes; this seems sensible, but it needs to be remembered that class distinction at the beginning of the last century was much stronger than it is today.

My mother never talked about her life in the factory, and I never knew in which factory she had worked (two of my uncles worked at different times at the big B.S.A. and Kynoch factories, and she never mentioned any connection with those, but Birmingham had a significant number of smaller factories involved in the manufacture of armaments and their components). No doubt she joined in the factory "singing while you work" – out of tune, for she could never sing in tune! She appeared to have savings at the time of her marriage in 1919, so she must have derived some benefit from this far from pleasant job, which she lost after the war ended. Fewer munitions were needed, and women who had worked in factories were now expected to yield to returning soldiers and to return to their pre-war roles. It seems strange in view of the dreadful carnage of the First World War, but many returning soldiers in the years following the armistice were in fact unemployed. An event in Leicestershire was a poignant example of this. In 1919-20, a house in Barwell was being built for a local manufacturer who had become rich during the war by supplying boots to the army. Unemployed ex-servicemen in the neighbourhood stormed the building, which had to be put under police protection. I also remember as a small child going shopping with Mum in the Coventry Road, in Small Heath, and there being usually two or three "Father Christmases" offering small toys from their bags for a few pence. At the age of three or four I couldn't understand this, but Mum told me they were all ex-servicemen. I was none the wiser!

This period – approximately 1915 to 1918 – formed the decisive years of my mother's life. There were three important changes. The first, and most important, is that she met my father, Harry Houghton. How they met I do not know. They married on 29 April 1919 at a double wedding in St John's Church, Ladywood, the other couple being Mum's cousin Cecil Darwood, and his wife, Muriel. The reception was held at Auntie Darwood's home, and Mum and Dad then went to live in his home in Small Heath, where they shared a three-bedroomed house with his parents and his then unmarried brother Fred, who was still suffering from a war wound.

Hilda's wedding in 1919

Secondly, the association with Cecil and Auntie Darwood's children changed Mum considerably. For the first time, she developed an interest in politics, and became a socialist. Will, the eldest son of the Darwoods, and his next brother, Cecil, were both living at home. Cecil, having been a scholarship boy at George Dixon Grammar School, had trained and become a schoolteacher. He was twenty-six and Will twenty-nine when they were both called up in 1916. They reported to the Warwickshire Regiment: both then refused to obey orders. This is a serious offence in the Army at any time: in wartime it can be punishable by death. They were court-martialled. They both refused to plead that they were pacifists, which they were not. They were socialists, and had refused to fight on behalf of the British Empire in an imperialist war. Whether this could carry the death penalty is not clear. Certainly men were being shot at the front for refusing to fight. But in 1916 the war was not as popular as it had been in 1914, when even my father, in a fit of patriotism, had tried to join up. (Fortunately for me, he was refused as he was a skilled worker and needed on the home front.) Will and Cecil were sentenced to imprisonment with hard labour, after which they were transferred to Dartmoor Prison for the rest of the war. Dartmoor was re-opened at this time to house over 1,000 conscientious objectors. It was named "Princetown Work Centre", with some men working in the prison and others being sent out to do farming or quarrying.

In 1919 Birmingham City Council would not accept Cecil as a teacher because of his war record. Both brothers were unemployed and unable to get work, but Cadbury's came to the rescue, and gave them jobs. As a Quaker firm, Cadbury's were supportive of people who had been conscientious objectors, including those who were not themselves Quakers. Birmingham appears to have been something of a centre for conscientious objection, partly supported by a strong local influence of both Quakers and socialists. Mum's cousins thrived at Cadbury's, with Cecil rising to a staff position in the sales department and becoming relatively wealthy. He later helped me a great deal, lent me books, and took me to a lecture by Harold Laski a famous political theorist in the Labour Party at one of the Selly Oak colleges. These colleges were assisted by Cadbury's, which was a powerful and benign influence in Birmingham for many years. I know that the stance taken by her two cousins during the war influenced Mum, and perhaps helped to further her marriage to a man who was a convinced socialist, and a former member of the Clarion Cyclists. The Clarion Cycling Club was a left-leaning organisation formed after a group of like-minded individuals got together in Birmingham in 1894. It took the Clarion name from Robert Blatchford's socialist newspaper. The club promoted both cycling and the Clarion, with cyclists often selling the newspaper on their outings. The club grew during the early 1900s with at one time more than 8000 members – many of them working class – and sections all over the UK. Later, I was a member of a Clarion choir organised by Katherine Thomson, the wife of the Marxist Professor of Classics at Birmingham, George Thomson.

In the December 1918 general election – the first one after the electoral franchise had been extended for women – Mum, like many of the women who had worked during the war, would not have been able to vote as she was under the age of thirty. My parents were later both ardent Labour voters, and my sister and I joined the gangs of kids jeering at their parents' political adversaries. Boys often broke into fights but we girls contented ourselves with chanting:

Vote, vote, vote for Freddie Longden,
Who's that knocking at the door?
If it's Mr Smedley Crooke
We'll hang him on a hook
And he won't come knocking any more.

Not that he ever did – he didn't need to. Like much of the rest of
Conservative Birmingham, our constituency – Deritend – usually
returned him. Freddie Longden took the seat for two years in
1929, but then had to wait until 1945 before he became the MP
again, by which time we had long left his constituency. In contrast,
Ladywood, where the Darwoods lived, was almost won for Labour
by Oswald Moseley in 1924, and in 1929 Moseley's previous agent,
Wilfrid Whiteley, who had been a conscientious objector in WW1,
took the seat for Labour for two years.

The third decisive event, which followed from Mum's employment in
the munitions factory, is that she met the woman who became my
Auntie Lily. Lily Hubbard was a member of a large impoverished
family living a few streets away from the Darwoods in Ladywood.
Mum and Lily became close friends, and Lily used to visit us often
after Mum's marriage, and so met Dad's brother – Uncle Fred, my
godfather. They married and had two children, Nellie and John,
cousins to whom I was close until their recent deaths.

The friendship of their two wives cemented the life long devotion
of the two brothers, the only children of my paternal
grandmother. Unhappily, the deprivation of Lily's early life
undermined her health – rheumatic fever in childhood left her with
a weakened heart – and she died at the age of fifty. Lily was long-
suffering, kind, gentle and cheerful whatever troubles came her
way, and we all missed her greatly.

Chapter 10: My mother remembered

After their marriage, my parents first lived with my father's parents, Harry and Ellen Houghton, and my Uncle Fred, in Small Heath. Mum, with her usual tactlessness, soon quarrelled with my grandmother, although in later years they got on well. In 1922, two years after my birth, my grandfather died, and the following year my grandmother and Uncle Fred went to live in what had been her family home near the city centre, as there was then only my great uncle, Jack, a builder, still living there. This left room for our growing family – Ralph joined us in 1923, and in August 1923 my sister Barbara was born. Then, in May 1929, my little brother Harry Esmond, always known to us as Esy, was born. We were all delivered at home, Mum being attended at all of the births by the local midwife, Mrs Bradley.

One of my earliest memories is being in floods of tears after Mum had scolded me for some childish peccadillo. She was worried: "Whatever is the matter?" she said. The reply horrified her. "My mummy doesn't love me," I stumbled out. She picked me up. "Of course I love you," she comforted me. I never doubted her love again and have reason to be grateful to her more times than I can remember. But I have realised that the incident illustrated one way in which she differed from the other mothers I knew and must have been the direct result of her own deprived childhood: she was not good at expressing her love for her children.

When I started school at the age of five, she took me there on the first day with a friend from further along the street, Doris Potter. Mrs Potter was a very busy woman as her father was the licensee of a small beer shop, but was too old to run it. So his daughter did that as well as caring for her three children, her policeman husband (who worked irregular hours) and her father. Mum therefore helped out by taking us both to start school, and after presenting us to the headmistress, merely deposited us: no farewell kiss. Later, I discovered that the other children were all kissed when brought to school even when they had been there for some weeks. Again, reflecting on my mother's childhood, I can see that she would have had no memory of being kissed as a child, and therefore did not find it natural.

On the other hand, I doubt if many of the other children were as well prepared for school as I was. Mum taught me to sing the alphabet as she had learnt it herself. Of course it was phonetics at school when we were learning to read, and at first this confused me, but I soon sorted that out. I could also count up to at least ten before I was five, knew the days of the week and the months of the year (the latter to a rhyme I still know). I knew the address of the house where we lived and could eat properly at the table. I have been an infant school governor, and I know that even today not all five year olds are as well prepared. I had actually been looking forward to school, though I had no idea what it would be like, but Mum made me think it would be fun, and it was. I hadn't been there more than a week or two when I was persuading Doris to hide outside when we returned from the midday break, and crawl back into our classroom (a curtained off section of the hall) and then astonish the class by suddenly appearing among them from under the curtain. There was no punishment; we were, though, reminded that it wasn't really a good idea because "Look at how dirty your hands are now!" I loved school, and I think this was largely due to Mum's preparation, for she had been happy at school, and had she been born in later times would certainly have continued her education.

Another way in which her early life affected the way in which she raised her own children was in her excellent food arrangements. In those days the street was our playground. Other kids used to go home from time to time for what they called "a piece" – a piece of bread. This was often spread with lard and sprinkled with sugar. I thought it revolting – Mum never provided such things. She did, however provide three good meals a day, and hot milk and a spoonful of cod-liver oil and malt at bedtime. The latter might have been from her knowledge of hospitals where she had worked, but I am sure that the strict meals routine was an echo of her own childhood, where she would have had food at meal-times with no snacks between.

In fact, she was quite a strict parent in many ways. Food had to be eaten at the table, which had to be properly laid – not the case in all working class homes at that time. Bedtime was also strictly adhered to. By eight o'clock we were tucked up in bed all the year round. In the summer my sister and I used to lie in bed listening to the cries of what we thought were luckier children, who played in the street until it was quite dark.

In the 1920's, and before my younger brother Esy, was born, we were among the better-off families in the street, as my father had more work than he could manage, and sub-employed sometimes two or three workmen. (This was a practice in small factories in Birmingham – it was dying out then and had disappeared completely by the end of the thirties.) Mum therefore had some extra money to spend, and she used this to take us on outings. She missed the countryside, and would often take Barbara, my sister, and me on a bus ride out of the city, or to a more distant park than our own Small Heath Park, where we were able to go unaccompanied by the time I was about nine or ten. When Uncle Alf's daughter Winnie lived with us for a time one summer we went on more outings than I can remember. Winnie was ailing and Mum's cousin Will (Auntie Darwood's son) suggested he take her to a very good doctor whom in knew in the Selly Oak area of the city. This luminary pronounced there was nothing to worry about: Winnie was outgrowing her strength! I don't know what my father said to Mum but the upshot was that at his insistence she then took Winnie to Dad's doctor. Dr Wilkinson was the son-in-law of old Dr Ravenhill, who had ministered to, and been much loved by, the residents of the slums of nineteenth century Birmingham. His surgery was some way from our house but until we moved to the outskirts of the city, he remained our doctor. So Mum went to his surgery with Winnie. Dad was right. Unfortunately Winnie had tuberculosis. The poor girl eventually died in the sanatorium at Yardley, aged just thirteen.

Hilda with Winnie (on left), Barbara, Connie, and a neighbour's son, in about 1927

Mum was very fond of animals. Bobby, our Pomeranian dog, lasted through most of my childhood. He lived for about twelve years. He was a thoroughbred, intended to be a show dog, but he grew to be a little over the regulation size for his breed. First, he had belonged to a neighbour, Mr Draper, my friend Doris's grandfather, who gave Bobby to me. Bobby was a coward: Mum used to take him with us to Small Heath Park, and let him off the lead to drink at the edge of the lake. Then he would scamper away, but returned very swiftly when he saw another dog! He would allow no-one but my father to comb his long black hair. My sister and I used to tease Bobby. We would glance through the kitchen window and shout "Cats!" Off he would run to chase them away and would be jumping up the high garden fence before he realised he had been tricked. Bobby then returned, growling, to his box in the kitchen and sulked.

We normally had at least one cat – in fact I can remember that we once had three. Mum used to take in strays, and when we lived in the inner city there were plenty of those. Sometimes these cats produced kittens, and Dad had the unpleasant task of drowning them before their eyes opened, because there was no vet in the area, and even if there had been I don't think Mum could have afforded the fee. Dad hated this. Later, when we had moved to an outer city suburb, Mum managed to find a hedgehog, and for a long time we had a tortoise too. When Ralph returned from army service in India with a monkey, Barbara was convinced he had brought it from India, but he had actually purchased it in England. Dad was very fond of the monkey, which used to sit on his shoulder. However, when he was left alone in the house the monkey screamed, neighbours complained, and eventually it had to go.

Mum worked hard, especially on Tuesday, which was for her washing day. The other women all washed on Monday. Mum chose to take life easy on Mondays and always made cakes in the afternoon. In those days washing was a long-drawn-out business of boiling whites, thumping other clothes in a tub, prolonged rinsings (which in the case of whites was in an infusion of Reckitt's Blue) and finally everything had to be put through the old-fashioned wringer, which stood in the garden, covered with a rainproof cloth. Turning the mangle was something I was often called upon to do. I hated it.

Mum's habit after the children had been packed off to school was to make a fresh pot of tea and settle down in the armchair in the kitchen with a book. Consequently, she never started the day's chores before ten o'clock, by which time the other women in the street would already have had the washing out on the clothesline. Mum never seemed to realise that it was an odd coincidence that I was regularly "kept in" by my teacher on washing day. Little did she know that I had sneaked round the back of the house and peered through the kitchen window. If she was still engaged in the last task of the washing, which was scrubbing my father's work overalls, I would disappear and return later when there were signs of tea in the kitchen. My response to her "Where have you been till this time?" was to always blame the teacher.

Books were more important to Mum than the washing. She read widely and quite indiscriminately. Dad thought no one after Dickens was worth reading and his collection of his books (which I still have) are well-thumbed, but the books Mum read – modern romances – have not survived.

Mum could cook, and though she hated housework she did it and the house was kept clean. She had worked as a cleaner when times were hard, and used to visit my great-uncle Jack to clean his rooms after Fred had moved elsewhere with his growing family. My sister and I usually accompanied her and often played in a bread cart, which was kept in the house's yard, and visited the horses and a donkey in the stables. When my great-grandfather lived there he had used the stables and some of the yard for his work – he was a coal merchant and the house was named *Cottage, Coal Yard*. Jack had subsequently used the yard for his building materials and equipment, although by this time – the late 1920's – he was elderly and working less. An elderly couple who sold rock salt owned the donkey. Later, the owner of the yard and its houses sold up, and Jack had to move to a smaller house nearby, but my mother still used to visit to clean for him. But although Mum was good at cooking and cleaning, she was no good at sewing. However, she tried, and occasionally made garments for Barbara and me, which we refused to wear. Once she purchased a sewing machine, but several broken needles and other disasters later she returned it to the shop and accepted two large vases instead. Fortunately, Auntie Darwood was an excellent dressmaker and made all our school dresses for Mum. Washing was one thing, but ironing was another. Mum had a large basket of back numbers, clean washing which never got as far as the ironing board. If we couldn't find a garment we wanted to wear that was the place to look for it!

But if Mum was a somewhat haphazard housewife, she was a great mother. I remember when April showers came our way we didn't wait for the flowers they bring in May: Mum made us go out into them, because she thought April rain was fun. If you don't see the foliage when it first appears you miss some lovely shades of green and Mum made us realise that – her favourite colour was spring green. She loved flowers and had discovered a house where bunches of flowers were sold from the garden. She frequently spent her last few pence on a Friday afternoon on a bunch.

My father loved his wayward wife, though he did criticise her choice of reading! He was a "steel toy maker" – a skilled workman making small metal objects by hand. This was an old Birmingham craft, but when I registered his death in Birmingham in 1975 the young registrar had never heard of the trade and I had to insist it was entered correctly on the certificate. In my early childhood, Dad used to make "rubber knives", a name that puzzled me greatly until I discovered they were used for tapping rubber trees for their latex sap. Native to South America, these trees were transferred to the then British colony of Malaya via Kew, and for a time were very important, providing tyres for the growing car industry. But synthetic rubber was invented and as its production increased there was less demand for the knives. In addition, Woolworth's stores started to sell cheap mass produced articles such as corkscrews and tin openers, with which the largely hand-made goods made by my father and his fellow workers could not compete. By the early thirties, Dad was now sometimes on short time, though never fully unemployed. Mum could no longer afford to pay a cleaning lady; in fact, she looked for work herself and for a time cleaned other people's homes. She had to be careful with the housekeeping money, but she managed very well, and we never went hungry. As a grammar school pupil I received a "maintenance" grant, but it was never used to supplement the housekeeping money. I always had the necessary uniform, books, tram fare, and even some pocket money. Mum showed the same enterprise during the war. She had located a farm about two miles away from the edge of the city where we lived and which was prepared to sell her an occasional chicken, "off the ration". Several times she walked to the farm and returned with a chicken, which she then proceeded to pluck and draw, while my sister and I looked on, horrified.

When the Second World War began, we were living on the outskirts of the city in King's Norton. Mum's first war job was working as a cook in a local canteen used by ARP (Air Raid Precautions) workers. She worked there with her friend Mrs Kunes (whom she had got to know because Stella Kunes and I had become friends at school). That didn't last long – one day they arrived home and sat shaking with uncontrollable laughter. They had both been sacked – Mrs Kunes for poor cooking, and my mother for cheek! My mother then joined the ARP. Dad had made the air-raid shelter in the garden reasonably comfortable, but except when on fire-watching duties – which were compulsory for most men who were not in the forces – he went to his bed throughout the blitz. But Mum was not with us in the shelter either, for she was now out in every air raid – as an ambulance attendant. She was extremely courageous at this time, and had learnt to drive in case the ambulance driver was injured. She was always cross with us when she came home in the mornings because we were usually still eating our breakfast in a leisurely manner, when we were supposed to have started the day's chores! Mum then set to and did them herself.

Mum suffered from depression at the end of the war, and spent a few weeks in a convalescent home, but the depression returned a few years later and she needed medical treatment. I believe this problem had its roots in her early life. There is no doubt in my mind that Mum was happy as long as she felt needed, and a sense of belonging. She frequently sought out relatives and visited them though they never came to see us. Dad, who had a secure family life as a child, though poor, didn't approve of this behaviour; he thought Mum was cheapening herself by appearing to be a "hanger on". He was stiff-necked in this way, but it was a matter of pride with him not to seem to be wanting anything from other people, family or not. On one occasion he was furious when Barbara and I thought we might as well have a free Christmas treat from the Salvation Army. We even went to the Tory treat when a neighbour gave us tickets, but Mum said we'd better not tell him! In fact, there were a number of things about which Mum said "Don't tell your father".

For example, Mum occasionally bought small food items from a local shop on what used to be called "the strap". This was nothing to do with a method of punishment; it meant running up small debts. She also ran an account at a small draper's shop run by a Miss Blackshaw. This was used mainly for the hair ribbons and other small items, which my sister loved. I was the one who was sent to pay small sums on account and strictly enjoined not to tell my father. I don't think he ever knew, though he might have wondered about the hair ribbons and gloves!

Hilda at the convalescent home, about 1949

Hilda and her son, Es

Hilda and Harry, about 1950

My mother taught me many things. But she did more than that – she made life seem fun. Her occasional bursts of anger were always short-lived. As many other parents did then, she had a cane, with which we were occasionally threatened, but it was never used. She used to say "I'll tell your father" when we were especially tiresome, but she never did. Nobody told him anything and he wouldn't have taken much notice if we had.

During her teens my sister developed kidney disease and was frequently hospitalized in subsequent years. She died when she was only thirty-five in 1958, an event which greatly distressed my mother. It was even more distressing to learn only one year after her death that kidney transplants were to become available. The disease that Barbara had – nephritis – is now fully curable if identified in its early stages. Mum nursed Barbara devotedly, but after her death Mum began to decline. However, before she died she and my father had achieved a few years of tranquil old age. They went on holidays in England – generally to seaside resorts, including Blackpool and Brixham – and they visited me and my children in High Wycombe several times. The children also went to stay with Mum: at last she felt needed again.

Mum had a heart attack when she was seventy-one. She was in hospital recovering from this when she suddenly suffered another one and died before medical aid could save her. I had been visiting the hospital every weekend, when my husband was able to look after our children. Dad phoned to say Mum was much better and they both thought I should have a weekend off this tiring journey to Birmingham. I didn't go. I have never forgiven myself. When the hospital returned the letter I had sent in lieu with "Deceased" scrawled across it, I was devastated.

Chapter 11: What became of the others in this story

This is primarily the story of my mother. But I cannot leave the people she knew, and her own life, without telling something of their histories.

Eliza Tedstone continued to live with the Darwoods in Birmingham until her death in 1918. In 1909, when she was in her late eighties, she would have been eligible to receive the newly introduced old age pension and it seems likely that she would have been one of those who queued up at the post office to be issued with a claim form in the later months of 1908.

One of the early actions of the 1906 Liberal Government was the introduction of old age pensions. Ministers such as Lloyd George hated the poor law and wanted to guarantee at least a minimum wage for poor people too old to work, faced as they were with either the workhouse or the charity of relatives. The harshness of conditions for working people had been challenged by social investigators such as Charles Booth and Seebohm Rowntree who showed that many working people were almost destitute at some time in their lives, and that the plight of elderly women was particularly severe, with many dependent on relatives, as was Eliza, or obliged to continue in very low income employment to survive. As the historian Eric Hobsbawm wrote: "When workers lost their employment – which they might do at the end of the job, of the week, of the day or even of the hour – they had nothing to fall back upon – except their savings, their friendly society or trade union, their credit with local shopkeepers, their neighbours and friends, the pawnbroker or the Poor Law … When they grew old or infirm, they were lost unless helped by their children, for effective insurance or private pension schemes covered only a few of them. Nothing is more characteristic of working-class life, and harder for us to imagine today, than this virtually total absence of social security."

The new pension scheme provided a small weekly pension and was means-tested. The introduction of pensions was supported by working class organizations, such as trade unions, and many churches and individuals of standing. A strong supporter was George Cadbury in Birmingham. In 1901 he had purchased a newspaper – *The Daily News* (whose first editor had been Charles Dickens) – and used it to campaign against sweated labour, and for old age pensions.

In 1908 the *Manchester Guardian* reported steadily increasing applications by old people for the new single person's pension of five shillings weekly, and the couples' pension of seven shillings and sixpence. There was a form to fill in (often the old people needed help with this, as would have Eliza), giving simple information such as name and address and date of birth. Applicants had to be at least seventy years old, and there were grounds for disqualification, which included imprisonment during the last ten years without the option of a fine, people who were habitually drunk, or who had never worked when able to do so or who were otherwise of bad character. People who had received Poor Law relief in the preceding year were also disqualified. Applications were verified by the Inland Revenue or by Poor Law officials, who made home visits. Some officials appear to have done their best to support the applications. For instance, a Jewish applicant in Manchester was asked to produce his naturalization papers, but they could not be found. He was then asked whether he had ever voted in an election in this country. He had, and duly received the pension.

After all this, applicants still had to appear before a committee. One "very tidy-looking" old couple had difficulty in mounting the steps into the Town Hall in Manchester, but they made it. One wonders how many didn't, for it is known that not all eligible old people managed to assert their claim. Eliza would have had to visit the Birmingham Council House, no doubt accompanied by Auntie Darwood or Uncle Ben. On January 1st 1909, more than half a million people became the first OAPs, with Eliza almost certainly being one of them. They were the lucky ones. Though some people, like Eliza, lived far beyond the minimum age of seventy, on the whole people in the early twentieth century were not as long-lived as we have since become.

Eliza lived to a great age – her death certificate gave her age as 102, although earlier records suggest that she may have been about five or more years younger than this (unless she lied to her younger husband about her age!) Mum also recalled that during the First World War, Eliza used to complain about "our government" letting "those things over here". She was referring to Zeppelin raids over Birmingham. The Black Country and Birmingham experienced a significant amount of bombing from German Zeppelins (air-ships) towards the end of the First World War. The earliest memory of the Birmingham based artist Norman Neasom was a night in October 1917 when he was carried into his parents' bedroom to see the searchlights over Birmingham through the windows of their Worcestershire farmhouse as a German Zeppelin tried to bomb the Austin motor works. Newspapers carried regular reports of deaths and destruction cause by Zeppelins in other areas, particularly London, the South and the East Coast. They were not efficient bombing planes, and the damage they inflicted was minimal compared with later bombing in World War Two.

Nevertheless, at the time they must have been terrifying and they clearly made a big impression on Eliza.

Although Eliza lived long enough to know of the legislation in March 1918 which extended the right of women to vote, she didn't quite live long enough to see the end of the war or her daughter voting in the next election at the end of that year. Nevertheless, a hundred years, approximately, was a very good age for a countrywoman who had lived a mainly impoverished and hard life.

More details of Eliza's early life were given in an article that was in the Birmingham Gazette on 13th January 1917, when she received a prize of five guineas for being their oldest reader. The reporter found that although some of her faculties were failing she still took an active interest in her surroundings and had the paper read to her every day by her daughter (hence, presumably, her anger about the Zeppelin raids). She recounted how she had been born in the year of the Battle of Waterloo and that her mother had died shortly after birth. She was then brought up by a Mrs Duckett, and known by that surname. This caused some confusion as she needed evidence of her birth in order to get the prize, but the Gazette made enquiries at Condover Church and found a record of a baptism in the name of "Duckett". Eliza's actual surname was "Prinn", as shown not only on her marriage certificate but also on the birth registrations of her first two illegitimate children. She told the reporter about her early life – about times when the price of bread was prohibitively high, but attributed her good health and long life to having lived plainer and worked harder in the old days. She also commented that people were healthier in the old days (although the premature deaths in Perry Gutter of Sarah and various children rather contradict this). She also remembered being in service as a nurse when young and travelling by coach with her mistress to London, and seeing a railway engine for the first time.

Auntie Darwood, long widowed, continued to live at 106 Rann Street Ladywood until she died in 1948. In our youth, my sister and I spent many weekends with her and her youngest daughter Lucy, who never married and lived with her mother nearly all her life. Lucy used to take us out, often to the cinema, or to nearby "Blackpool", the name given to the reservoir which the Municipal Authority had made into a local resort, complete with artificial sands. Auntie Darwood was like a grandmother to us. She taught me many things – for instance, how to make gravy, not, as nowadays, artificially, but as it was made by the cooks in *Uncle Tom's Cabin*. Auntie Darwood also taught me how to cut out a dress – not, I'm afraid, very successfully, though I did buy patterns and very cheap material from Lewis's huge store in Birmingham, in which a whole floor used to be given over to dressmaking materials and patterns. Auntie Darwood hardly knew my paternal grandmother, who was older than she, but always asked me how she was and added, in her Shropshire accent which never left her "'er's marvellous". Auntie Kitty's only son Donald lived with Auntie Darwood, attended George Dixon Grammar School and then trained to be a chartered accountant. I don't think he ever practised that profession as he joined the army just before the outbreak of war, and became a Lieutenant Colonel before it ended. He lived in London in later life, and we lost touch.

Auntie Darwood

Uncle Harry, Mum's older half-brother, continued to live in
Wolverhampton all his life. He worked as a carter as a younger
man, later moving into work on buses. Both Martha's husband
William and their son-in-law worked as carters for the corporation,
so it seems that Harry followed in their footsteps and was well
settled in his new life there after leaving his first family home in
such sad circumstances. Later in life he was a ticket inspector on
the city buses. He outlived his wife Maud. They had no children
and he gave her jewellery to his sister Kitty, who gave me one of
the brooches, which I still have.

Kitty became a nurse. In later years she took on private nursing and eventually nursed a wealthy young man who suffered from tuberculosis. His father, an industrialist in West Bromwich, had died. Mrs Hughes, his mother, went to live in the South of France, leaving her son in the care of my aunt and their Irish maid Maggie. Because the house was entailed, the son married my aunt so that when he died she inherited the quite large house, though not much money. For some years she ran it as a nursing home. My father was quite friendly with Kitty in his old age and they visited one another occasionally. Kitty wrote to me when my mother died, a wonderful letter of sympathy and love. However, when Kitty died I had left the Birmingham area and unfortunately we were not informed of her death, only realising some time later that it had happened when we saw a newspaper report of Maggie having been found dead in an empty house, where she had been living alone.

Finally, what of Alf, Mum's brother, who, designated like her "a pauper", shared her workhouse life for some years? At about fourteen he was found work as a farm labourer in North Wales, and it was when doing this work that he met his father once, and for the last time. After a few years Alf moved to the south of Wales and worked for several years in the Margam steel works. He married in 1914 and during the First World War he served in the Army Cyclists Corps.

In later years I knew my uncle well as at one time he and his family shared our home in Birmingham. I versified his story as follows:

> A workhouse boy, in his restricted childhood
> Alf never explored the hills and vales
> Of his native Shropshire.
> At fourteen the "Guardians" found him work;

Labouring, unskilled, alone somewhere in North Wales.
Here, for the first and last time since childhood
Alf met his father. Charles claimed no recognition.
A casual worker, he addressed the young labourer as "Sir".
Sadly, and with customary melodrama, Alf declared
"So it has come to this."
He left the farm, the area, the work,
He left the land and found a different lifestyle.
Travelled to South Wales and settled down,
Joining the throng at the Margam Steel Works.
Married, a son and daughter,
Even acquired a house; a home at last.
Alf was happy there.
But not for long. 1916 found him in the trenches.
Back in a grateful country, Alf returned to his work.
In the late twenties, slump descended on the country;
The steel works closed, and Alf was unemployed.
South Wales became known as a depressed area.
A visit from the Prince of Wales, and his famous words,
"Something must be done", resulted in .. nothing!
Sister Hilda, in Birmingham, gave shelter to Alf's family.
Cousin Frank gave him a garage job.
The garage failed; back on the dole went Alf.
Alf's daughter died. He hid his grief.
Losing a child? The common lot of many.
The years passed. In time, Alf's country needed him again.
Too old to fight,
But not too old to make the means of fighting.
B.S.A. – Birmingham Small Arms.
Here Alf worked at the city's oldest trade.
War brought blitz.
When the characteristic "er, er, er" of German planes

Sounded from the sky, many died;
Alf and his wife survived.
Their house did not; "bombed out" they called it,
As inner city dwellers walked in their hundreds
Four, five, six miles to escape the bombs.
After the war, Alf was growing old.
Still hoping that something would "turn up"
Alf took to firing a weekly bullet,
A John Bull bullet, in the weekly
Contest to cap a short verse with a witty last line.
Alas, Alf was a jovial, kindly man, but not witty!
One last throw for happiness remained.
Alf found "another woman"!
No young beauty she, a woman old and bent.
Bearing, like Alf, the scars of age and toil.
Now Alf acquired a new name:
His Welsh wife's name for him,
We began to call him "the old bugger".   "
We all loved the old bugger.
He loved children and they loved him.
Alf sometimes forgot to pay his debts,
But he never forgot
To share a joke, or a bag of sweets
With the children.

The people in this book are all long gone. I am now the granny in
the family! But I hope and believe that my children and
grandchildren have inherited something of my mother's
indomitable spirit, and that they, and others, will enjoy reading
about her life. I owe her more than I can express.

Hilda at the wedding of her daughter, Barbara, in 1946

Hilda at the wedding of her daughter, Connie, in 1951

Bibliography

Beddoes Connection in Hopesay, anon, pamphlet purchased in Hopesay

Mr Kipling's Army, Byron Farwell, 1981

The Workhouse Cookbook, Peter Higginbotham, 2008

Life in the Victorian and Edwardian Workhouse, Michelle Higgs, 2007

Industry and Empire: The Birth of the Industrial Revolution, Eric Hobsbawm, 1968

A Shropshire Lad, A.E. Housman, 1896

The King's Shropshire Light Infantry, J.R.B. Moulsdale, 1972

How The Old Age Pension Was Won, National Pensioners Convention, 2006

Rural Englands, Barry Reay, 2004

Shropshire Family History Journal, Shropshire Family History Society

Holly Mount, Tottington – A Labour of Love, John Slawson, 1995

South West Shropshire Historical and Archaeological Society Journal, SWSHAS (with particular reference to three articles by Alan Goff about the Clun Poor Law Union)

Shoemaking, June Swann, 2008

My Ancestor was an Agricultural Labourer, Ian H. Waller, 2007

The Story of Army Education 1643 – 1963, Colonel A.C.T. White, 1963